RATIONAL EMOTIVE BEHAVIOR THERAPY

ALBERT ELLIS

RATIONAL EMOTIVE BEHAVIOR THERAPY
IT WORKS FOR ME—
IT CAN WORK FOR YOU

Prometheus Books

59 John Glenn Drive
Amherst, New York 14228-2197

Published 2004 by Prometheus Books

Inquiries should be addressed to
Prometheus Books
59 John Glenn Drive
Amherst, New York 14228-2197
VOICE: 716-691-0133, ext. 207
FAX: 716-564-2711
WWW.PROMETHEUSBOOKS.COM

08 07 06 05 04   5 4 3 2 1

Library of Congress Cataloging-in-Publication Data

Ellis, Albert.
    Rational emotive behavior therapy : it works for me—it can work for you /
Albert Ellis.
        p. cm.
    Includes bibliographical references and index.
    ISBN 1-59102-184-7 (pbk. : alk. paper)
    1. Rational emotive behavior therapy. 2. Ellis, Albert—Mental health.
3. Psychotherapists—United States—Biography. I. Title.

RC489.R3E4648 2004
616.89'14—dc22

2004003664

Printed in the United States of America on acid-free paper

To

Debbie Joffe

who helped greatly in gathering the materials
for and putting together this book

and to the hundreds of people that I have helped and read
about who marvelously coped with
their disabilities and emotional problems.

CONTENTS

CONTENTS

ACKNOWLEDGMENTS

Emmett Velten, Kevin E. FitzMaurice, and Debbie Joffe read early versions of this manuscript and made valuable suggestions. Tim Runion worked with the book in many ways to give it excellent order. Many thanks!

1.

INTRODUCTION:
THE BEGINNINGS OF MY COPING
WITH MY DISABILITIES

In some respects, you could say that I was born with a tendency to become disabled, but that I was also born with a tendency to cope with disability. Of course the two tendencies may be reciprocal. People like me who have serious disabilities, especially from their early life onward, to some extent *have to* cope with them and may develop considerable coping ability. On the other hand, other people with severe physical problems frequently give up, whine and scream, and make themselves uncoping and dependent.

Let me say at the start what I shall emphasize in this book. Psychosomatic explanations or emotional reasons for human behavior only partly explain why and how we act. Sigmund Freud and his followers brilliantly devised such explanations.

For instance, I hypothesized in the preceding paragraph that I was frequently disabled and *therefore* I learned or taught myself to cope with disability. Perhaps. I also could have reached the conclusion that *since* I had to cope with disability from an early age, I *therefore* pursued intellectual instead of physical pursuits and focused on making myself into a writer. Again, perhaps!

Alfred Adler, a non-Freudian but still an analyst, might add another "reason": I felt so inferior because of my disabilities that I compensated for them and made myself into a writer of many books.

The trouble with this kind of psychodynamic explanation is that it *sounds* much truer than it often is. There are, of course, several other reasons why I could have become a writer. For example: (1) My mother was a poor writer and pushed me to make up for her defects. (2) My brother was better at sports than I was, so writing became my "sport." (3) One of my junior high school teachers thought I had a great ability at writing and insisted that I be an author. (4) One of my college teachers said that I was so good at writing that even though I made several grammatical errors, I would definitely be good enough to become published and would have competent editors correct my grammar. (5) I had a natural talent for both writing and speaking. I chose writing over selling as a career when I noticed that my father—although a great salesman— was also an exaggerator and dishonest, so I chose writing as an "honest" profession.

All these psychodynamic explanations may have some degree of truth. But some of them may also be quite false. So let me be cautious about making such interpretations—particularly since I am a therapist, and I think that therapists are often too loose and misleading in their psychodynamic explanations. However brilliant and logical their interpretations may seem and how solidly their clients may agree with them, please listen, watch out, and check their accuracy.

I had some formidable disabilities as a child, and I think I coped with them damned well. But let me not exaggerate. Yes, I was prone to being sicker than most children, but I was also born and reared with several health advantages. I had high energy and the inclination to use it. Even when I was sick, I was active. In fact, all my life I have hated inactivity and done my best to avoid it. Sleep and relaxation just do not suit me.

For example, when I was four years old my mother had me nap every afternoon for, presumably, a couple of hours. Maybe she wanted to get rid of me, along with my younger brother and younger sister. Or maybe, as I learned during my hospital stay a year later, it was customary for people to put children down for an afternoon nap. Presumably, as the nurses at the hospital explained, they needed it.

Not I! When my mother or the nurses put me in my crib, I stubbornly refused to doze off. I just wasn't tired—and I had better things to do. Preferably, I would have liked to talk to my friends, romp outside my house, play a game, or do some other activity. But since that was against the rules, I graciously lay in my bed for a required hour or two and did what I could to be mentally active. I thought and I fantasized. As I recall, my thinking was mainly practical. My problems weren't deep, but real. How could I get back in school when we moved from Pittsburgh to New York, knowing they wouldn't let me back in school for another year or so? What games would I like to play and with whom could I play them? How could I stop my sister from crying so much? How could I make some new friends? These were problems, and I wanted to solve them in advance, without waiting for them to arise. Figuring out solutions to problems was interesting! I enjoyed it. It kept me from being bored. It was active.

Come to think of it, coping with illness was also being active. Yes, active. I had the usual childhood diseases—like measles and mumps—and they mainly tended to require bed rest. But not *sleep* rest. Sleep itself was something of a nuisance, since it stopped me from *doing*. I always awoke eager to *get going*. I didn't hate sleeping, and I even enjoyed most of my dreams. But, jack-in-the-box that I was, I hated the time out from living that went with sleep. So when I was in bed with an illness, I coped with the resting by thinking and fantasizing. That *was* truly coping; and since thinking was highly enjoyable, it made me a happy coper—which sidetracked the pain of the illness itself.

This leads me to a tentative—highly tentative—conclusion. Activity is my thing. Not physical activity. I am definitely not a jock, runner, boxer, football player, wrestler, workout artist, or anything like that. My physical talents were decent in my childhood and adolescence, but waned as I passed twenty. Maybe because I wasn't very good at sports and therefore gave them up. Or maybe they were just too physically demanding.

The one exception that lasted into my eighties, when finally my legs became wobbly and I had to give it up, was walking. Up to that time I was a very good and fast walker. I often preferred walking to riding the bus in New York, because I could often beat the bus—and I hate to waste time.

Oh! Again, I just thought of it. Walking is action, all right. But with me, when I am in good shape, it is double action. I can walk and think at the same time. With most physical activity, I have to concentrate pretty fully on my body and what it is doing. And on the sport. But I dote on being active, with light physical exercise—say walking or Ping-Pong—and with all kinds of mental gymnastics—especially plotting, scheming, planning, and prophylactic anticipating. I used to, as I shall tell later, ruminatively worry, but I almost completely cured myself of that. I still think of bad things that might well happen—missing a plane connection, for example. But I figure out a contingency plan, and I never catastrophize or awfulize about even the worst possible scenarios. So I might even be dead. Too bad! To hell with it!

I like physical activity—going places, doing activities. And I like mental activity—thinking, planning, solving real-life problems. Games such as chess, bridge, and computer games are okay if I have nothing else to do. But since they have no real-life outcome, I rarely play them.

Ah, but I really enjoy the game of thinking about my misfortunes, handicaps, and disabilities. First, for its own sake—I like thinking and problem solving in itself. Second, I enjoy thinking for the good practical results I often get. Third, I like to figure out solutions to other people's problems. That's why I became a therapist and why, after sixty-one years, I am still playing the psychotherapist game. When people ask me what career I would choose if I were not a therapist, I reply that I would probably be an efficiency expert. I thoroughly enjoy encountering real-life difficulties.

For what reasons? I could again give several explanations or interpretations. But who the hell really knows? Personally, I favor several: (1) I have a natural talent for problem solving and I like exerting it. (2) From childhood onward I had more than my share of problem situations, so I was encouraged to solve them. (3) My father was a businessman who constantly solved economic issues and made money helping people (for his own good) solve theirs. (4) My brother, while physically excelling me, was also a great problem solver (and later national amateur chess champion). From my age of seven and his age of five, we delighted in solving problems together. (5) Oh, well, enough reasons!

No, I'd better consider one more possible reason. I was, let's face it, always intelligent in IQ terms. I consistently made advanced classes in school and did well in them. When they started giving us conventional IQ tests in junior high school when I was twelve, I invariably came out with the highest score—yes, of my special advanced and quite intelligent class. In my psychology class in college, I took the famous Army Alpha intelligence test and scored in the ninety-ninth percentile of thousands of testees. Usually, highly intelligent people like me dote on problem solving and are attracted to it.

For all the above reasons—and more—I reciprocally brought my problem-solving abilities to my disabilities *and* brought my disabilities to my problem solving. As Alfred Korzybski would say, "both/and, not either/or." This may not be a brilliant interpretation, but I think it is reasonably accurate.

But let's go back to my early disabilities. My mother tells me that I was a highly colicky baby who gave her great difficulty. I was was *her* disability, but I don't remember it at all.

I also inherited my father's proneness to allergies, but only vaguely remembered itching, like my father, more than my brother and sister. Perhaps they complained so much with hay fever, rose fever, sneezing from temperature changes, and what have you, that my allergic reactions were outnumbered and outshone. I don't remember myself as being especially allergic, even when I was afflicted with nephritis (kidney trouble) when I was four and a half. Many years later, I learned from my research that nephritis frequently involves allergic reactions.

The one ailment I dramatically remember preceded my nephritis by several weeks. I was playing in the lot across from our apartment on Bryant Avenue in the East Bronx—which was then a fairly upper-middle-class neighborhood—accompanied by my good friend Sidney, when my three-year-old brother (whom we were minding) accidentally dropped a rock on the little finger of my left hand.

I am damned sure it was an accident, though the psychoanalysts could really go to town in "interpreting" it. My brother, Paul, and I were always friendly, but who knows what deep-seated unconscious motives he had about my being older and bigger than he, and my paying much more attention to Sidney than to him. Paul was very contrite when he saw what damage the rock did to my finger. What seemed to be a flood of blood spurted out of it, and it felt completely numb. It looked like I would bleed to death had not Sidney quickly found a handkerchief, wrapped it around my pinky, and rushed me across the street to my mother, who then whisked me two blocks away to our family doctor.

I was somewhat in shock and was wholly focused on my rudely disrupted little finger—so focused that I hardly felt the pain. I was very curious about what the doctor would do; and although he was very reassuring, I imagined dire things like finger amputation. But I would interestedly wait and see.

Fortunately, the doctor bathed my finger in alcohol—which stung like hell—quickly sewed it up (very expertly, I thought), and put a large bandage on my small appendage. It was a miracle! The hurt was all gone. But a numbness remained for the next few weeks.

Now things get a little confusing here. A few weeks after my pinky got smashed, I was on my way to the first of my many visits to the hospital. Diagnosis: nephritis. Cause: presumably a streptococcus throat infection. Actually, I don't remember having a sore throat; but I do, of course, remember having a sore pinky. So at first I connected the bashed finger with the nephritis—and perhaps with the sore throat business. Apparently, there was no connection. But the doctors did say that my strep throat led to acute nephritis.

My first visit to the Presbyterian Hospital in Manhattan was for only a few weeks and included a tonsillectomy by a famous surgeon who later became Sen. Royal Copeland. I was told that with a few surgical strokes, he saved my life, for my tonsils were quite infected and, again, led to the nephritis. I appreciated my surgeon, but not the operation procedures. As I recall, I wasn't allowed to eat the night before surgery, and that wasn't so bad. But they deceived me otherwise.

I didn't mind the journey on a stretcher to the operating room. But just before surgery, they had me sniff a metal cone, which they said was an orange. Like hell it was! It was a cone filled with ether, and after a few sniffs, I was out, quite out.

I woke that afternoon in my hospital bed and this time I really had a sore throat. And ravishing thirst, which they refused to quench with water. Those nice pretty nurses, I thought, were really rotten bitches, not to mention lousy deceivers and water deprivers. I wasn't frightened, and I stood the pain and discomfort very well, but not the deception!

I lay boringly in my bed for a couple of days—comforted only by my thinking. My mother had two younger children at home, so I saw little of her. My father, throughout all my illnesses, was busy working. The other kids in the children's ward were newborns or younger than I. No real socializing occurred with them. So I thought and thought and thought—and fantasized about good things that had come or hopefully would. I was relatively frustrated, but not miserable.

Well, here we go again with reciprocal causes and effects. I was not depressed in these highly frustrating circumstances because I managed to think and fantasize my way into mental activity. Great! But I also was pushed by boring conditions that were foisted on me and forced me to resort to more pleasant thinking and fantasizing. I chose to think instead of passively let myself be bored. But conditions—my operation and lying in bed alone—largely influenced my resorting to active thinking— heredity *and* environment, both/and—as it almost always seems to be!

So it goes. Disability, restriction, and frustration of physical action from my early life onward encouraged me to take mental action. But I—yes, I—took the action. Like practically all humans, I am a constructivist and, when faced with Adversity (A in the ABCs of REBT) I have a real *choice* of how to feel and act at point C, my Consequence of Adversity (A). At point B (my Belief System), I can think Rational Beliefs (RBs) and tell myself, "I don't like A but I can deal with it and ameliorate it, and it is *not* catastrophic and awful if I can't change it!" If I have these RBs at B, I will then feel the Consequence (C) of *healthy* negative emotions—such as sorrow, regret, frustration, and annoyance. Good!

If I *also* choose to hold strong Irrational Beliefs (IBs) at point B, I will usually produce Consequences (C) of *unhealthy* (unproductive and destructive) feelings as my Consequences (C), such as anxiety, depression, and rage. So I partly have a *choice* of how to feel about Adversities.

My sister, Janet, had some of the physical disabilities—such as allergies to food and to weather changes—that I had. But she seemed to have more and stronger IBs *about* her Adversities (A). So from early childhood onward she partly chose IBs ("It's awful! Life is no good! I can't stand it!") that led her to have *unhealthy* feelings of depression, anger, and anxiety at point C (Consequence).

My brother, Paul, had serious allergies that led to convulsive sneezing when conditions changed from hot to cold, or vice versa. But his Adversities (A) did *not* lead him to be unhealthily miserable (C) but may have led to his quite rebellious and psychopathic behavior (C). Unlike my sister, he *chose* to be unmiserable and like myself was much happier than she.

My first major physical disability, then, was chronic nephritis, which I had from my fifth to my ninth year. All told, it sent me to the Presbyterian Hospital eight times—once for a period of ten months. During that time, as I shall report in more detail, I was on a strict (ungourmet) diet (for many weeks ate little but tomato and lettuce sandwiches). I was restricted from active sports (including handball, which I loved). I lost a year's schooling (which I considered a great deprivation). Other boys I encountered often considered me a weakling and a sissy.

Real Adversities and hassles! And no end in sight, since I

wasn't pretty sure that my nephritis was over until I was nine, and I was then given a clean bill of health by my doctors.

How did I take my physical troubles and restrictions? Pretty damned well. I disliked them but remained a happy child. I think I was happy *because* I coped well. I practically never whined and cried. I accepted what I couldn't change. I *created*, as I have been indicating, good substitute enjoyments—mainly mental ones. I habituated myself, consciously but without too much stressing, to coping mechanisms. By taking the *challenge* of doing so, I thereby mostly *enjoyed* my coping.

My reasons for being happy, however, not only stemmed from my congratulating myself because I coped so well. The coping *itself* stopped me from being miserable—as rational coping statements (or philosophies) usually do. *Then* my natural tendency for being happy—which I think I definitely had—as both my father and my mother had, gave me the leeway to shine through.

Coping statements *themselves* also often lead to happiness—because they include alternate plans. Thus, I told myself, "Yes, this damned nephritis is a restricting problem and bad. But not *too bad* or *terrible*. And through being hospitalized for it, I'll learn some new things about myself, look forward to future health, and after a few weeks be able to enjoy activities like playing ball, going to school, and conversing with Sid and my other friends." With this kind of rational coping, I unpessimistically looked forward to real enjoyments and was not merely unmiserable but happy. This is because I didn't blame myself, Albert, for my condition, nephritis.

Never, "*I* am bad for what I did. I am a worthless, undeserving *person*." The world—or fate, or what you will—was pretty depressing. But I still deserved life and happiness. I was sometimes guilty about my *acts*, rarely about my *self*. When I read Alfred Korzybski many years later, I instantly saw that he was correct: No one *is* her or his behavior. People wrongly think and follow the *is* of identity. Humans frequently act inhumanely. But no human *is* subhuman. Or superhuman. I am still a bit puzzled when so many of my quite intelligent clients have trouble fully seeing this.

No, I am not a depressive. I just felt depressed briefly and lightly about my nephritis (and headaches, as I'll explain later) during my childhood. Not even during my adolescence or adulthood was I clinically depressed. Of course, I still ask myself, "*Why*, with my long history of illness and disability, am I not a severe depressive? Many equally afflicted people would be. Why not I?"

As usual, I have no complete answer to this question, although I am a well-respected psychologist who helps people with their depressive tendencies. For there is—as yet—*no* complete answer. If I were severely depressed about the Adversities of my life—as indeed my sister, Janet, almost always was—it would be because of heredity *and* environmental influences. I would be born and raised to take misfortunes (like physical disabilities) too seriously and to berate myself for my failings, just as Janet steadily did. Not, fortunately, I!

2.

MY BOUT WITH
SEVERE HEADACHES

My bout with severe headaches began about the same time I was afflicted with nephritis. I was always prone to sudden, piercing headaches that would last a day or two and only temporarily keep me from productive activity. Then, with aspirin, cold presses on my temples, and other devices, the headaches went away for two or three weeks. Eventually they returned.

While they lasted—usually before bedtime, until I, with the help of the aspirin, went to sleep—they were pretty bad: piercing, throbbing, hot cheeks and temples, and other intense pains.

I took them well enough even though, unlike nephritis, they lasted—steadily lasted—till I was in my sixties. We never could find their specific origins, though I explored every possible source. No, they didn't seem to be from sinus trouble—which struck when I was twenty-eight and dissipated when I

had a Cauldwell-luc window operation and one other operation on my nose. These procedures helped my serious sinus
problems, but not the blasted headaches.

I read the medical literature and tried everything: other
analgesics besides aspirin, exercise, different sleep patterns,
and all kinds of diets and restrictions of suspicious foods.
Nothing worked. Steady headaches persisted for sixty years.

When I was seven and hospitalized for nephritis for ten
months, my hospital doctors were sure the headaches were
caused by gastrointestinal upsets and (unfortunately) tried a
drastic measure that was surely invented by the devil: rectal
irrigation of my lower intestine with tons—well, to be honest
about it, only gallons—of water. Every day at 11 AM, in spite of
my excuses (and I tried several), I endured the irrigation.
Come hell or high—very high—water.

After two months of this torture, I cried a halt to it, threat-
ening to get up and leave the hospital. Did all that irrigation
do me, my lower intestine, or my headaches, any good? No.
Did it aggravate the headaches? Probably, though my violent
protests may have done that, too.

Despite these protests, every day including Sundays, a cart
would be pushed up to my bedside and the treatment begun.
I am not sensitive to pain, but as a child I whined about it. To
this day, as in the dentist's office, I shut my mouth and am a
"good patient." So when the large nozzle and hose was put up
my anus, I bore it, bore the hot water going through me, felt it
inject into my lower and upper intestines, and thoroughly
hated every minute of its twenty-minute invasion of my intestinal privacy. I vividly remember this hot-water invasion to this
very day, eighty-three years later!

Normally, I would have liked the attention of the pretty nurses who gently guided my inner bath. I might well have made something sexual about it—as I did (as I have told in another autobiographical book) when they bathed my outer body. But the daily anticipation and actual discomfort of this intestinal horror drove all sexual ideas from my mind—until twenty minutes later.

Was I frightened every time the medical cart rolled up to my bedside for its fiendish "mercy" mission? Not exactly. I was not anxious, thought of nothing catastrophic, but was extremely frustrated—and angry at the misled torturers. Normally, I liked them and felt very friendly toward them. Not for those dreadful two months! I hoped they'd all drop dead, along with, at times, my mother, who passively went along with all doctor orders, in spite of my strongly urging her to intervene. Not a chance. So I was often angry at her, too.

I felt no anxiety or panic, then, nor fear of dying of this torture. I did, however, feel anger to the second or third degree. Like most people all over the world, I didn't cope too well with my anger because I thought it was entirely justified. Those doctor rascals, against my consent, inflicted this torture on me—and, of course, *they* made me angry. This was some nine years before I reached the age of sixteen and became devoted to philosophy and to reason. This was some thirty-three years before I started to invent rational emotive behavior therapy (REBT), at the age of forty, when I reviewed the major philosophers to see what they advocated regarding rage and other forms of emotional disturbance. So I justified my rage, thought the doctors had *made me* angry, and didn't consider *justified* anger a problem. Anxiety, yes; depression, yes. Because they made *me* uncomfortable, they did little good and much harm. But not anger.

Today, of course, I would have almost immediately seen the folly of my rage, fully acknowledged that *I* largely created it—after the doctors, of course, unfairly and "inexcusably" tortured me—and I would get right to work minimizing it and feeling *healthfully* sorry and frustrated instead. Why? Because REBT holds that even justified anger is self-defeating and usually leads to poor physical and social results.

Today, noticing my anger, I would forcefully and emotionally dispute it—Disputing Irrational Beliefs (IBs) is the D stage that follows the ABCs of REBT. So today I would vigorously Dispute my IBs leading to my rage: "My doctors are wrong—dead wrong—in prescribing these very uncomfortable enemas. They think they are right and they possibly may be. But even if they're wrong, they have a right, as fallible humans, to be wrong. I'm very sorry if they're wrong and are putting me through needless hassles. But again, if I really see that they have a right to be wrong, I'll be *only* sorry and not angry. Too damned bad, but it's not *awful!*"

If I had known my REBT—at the age of seven, no less!—I would have used it to rid myself of my anger. But I didn't know it, of course, and therefore stayed angry—until after two months they stopped "torturing" me.

I did cope with the doctors, my painful enemas, and partly with my anger, however, by adhering to my pre-REBT philosophy. I largely convinced myself that this horror, too, would pass—especially if I complained enough about it and kept pointing out to my doctors that, if anything, my headaches were worse after the enemas began. "Much worse," I lied—and thought that that might do the trick. Maybe it did. The "torture" soon stopped. Free at last from the turmoil of my guts!

But not at all free of the headaches. They were a little less frequent and intense once the stupid enemas stopped. But only a little. Still no cause was diagnosed, no matter how I (and others) tried to find it. Finally, after suffering from fierce headaches for more than sixty years, I figured out the probable cause. I was diagnosed as having type 1 insulin-dependent diabetes when I was forty-five. I strictly followed my diabetic regimen, but I was able to keep my blood sugar fairly low beginning only in the 1970s when I was in my sixties and when accurate blood sensors became available. I soon regularly kept my blood sugar close to 100, by testing my blood ten times a day (or more) and eating small meals— also ten times a day—around the clock.

What do you know! My headaches almost entirely disappeared, and since then I have experienced only infrequent mild ones. I have therefore figured out, and received some confirmation from my diabetologist, that the main cause of my frequent and fierce headaches was the hyperglycemia (high blood sugar) that I had, and was diagnosed as having, from at least my twenties onward, and quite possibly before.

Let us hope so! Ever since I have kept my blood sugar close to normal, my damned fierce headaches ceased. What a relief! After almost sixty years of headaches—now I had almost none for the last thirty years or so. Bless the modern blood sugar sensors!

Anyway, how did I emotionally handle my long years of headaches? At first, like my anger at my doctors, not very well. Here I was, a nice good boy who deserved great health—and the crummy headaches struck! Again: Here I was, doing my best to research the causes of the headaches—and again, no luck. "Unfair! Terrible!" I was mad at the headaches, even though I knew they hardly *deliberately* afflicted me, and knew I could not in the least make them suffer for their iniquity. But I was mad at them and at the cruel world. Now I realize how silly—and useless—my anger was.

Worse, I made myself somewhat depressed. Normally, I do not give up hope on almost anything. But as the headaches continued to blare away at my temples, I could not see them coming to an end, especially when my temples were relentlessly throbbing. In between headache outbreaks, I was my old optimistic self and didn't obsessively worry about their returning. For a week or two or three I was without them and assumed the best instead of the worst—that they would stay away a long time.

So I went about my regular enjoyable business—at school, at work, socially, sexually, writing all kinds of fiction and nonfiction, including songs and humorous verse. I never really let my headaches stop me—except for a fiendish night or so when they were piercing and when the only surcease from focusing on them was greatly welcomed sleep. As I have previously reported, sleep was usually not my cup of tea. However, the time it took out from headaches was most welcome.

Hence, I sometimes got myself depressed about the headaches. Life was no joy when they were in full force—and no end seemed in sight. Though never very religious—despite my history of steady Sunday School attendance—I prayed to God to relieve my bad headaches, and promised Him I would be a real good boy if He did. When He did—or something else ended my headache—I forgot about God and my promises to Him. After I became an atheist at the age of twelve, I forgot about God completely.

Sometimes, though rarely, I thought that life with piercing headaches wasn't worth continuing. Although I didn't think of killing myself, I would have been rather glad to quietly die in my sleep. On a number of times I have been deeply sad about losses, particularly woman friends whom I lost. But with the continued outbreak of ravaging headaches during my childhood, I came as close to feeling depressed as I ever came. It was moderate, not severe, depression that was brief.

To deal with this temporary depression, I used mild and nonelegant disputing and rational coping statements: "Maybe my headaches won't go on forever." "What can I use to distract myself while my headaches are bursting out?" "If I live long enough, maybe I can do some great things and enjoy renown."

Notice, from these kinds of statements, I wasn't depressed because of putting *myself* down. That rarely occurred to me. Even when I did something stupid, weak, or immoral, I automatically thought, "It was *bad* what I *did*." "But" I added, "I'm okay even though I did it." I used Eric Berne's philosophy years before I really knew it so I didn't have to work very hard at changing my depressive tendencies.

Fortunately, I didn't easily whine about my Adversities; and I didn't put myself down for failing to overcome them. Also, as I keep noting, I am an *active* coper. When afflicted by Adversities, I *determinedly* try to solve them. And I *stubbornly refuse* to denigrate me, my self, when I screw up. My anti-self-defaming is partly innate and partly figured out and self-taught. I work like hell at not damning myself, though I also strive to face my mistakes and failings. Why? Because I love serenity and hate hating myself. How come? For a variety of innate and acquired reasons.

So it took fairly extreme Adversities—my steady severe

headaches—to make me (or, rather, make myself) feel hopeless and depressed. Who wouldn't be? Damned few! Even Martin Seligman's rats, when faced with a problem that they couldn't solve, frequently depressed themselves. But not *always*. Even rats are unique individuals.

I made myself, as a child, somewhat depressed for a while, about my headaches or perhaps—I don't specifically remember anything else—other things. Then I returned to my natural problem solving and actively enjoying self. I reestablished some *hope* of overcoming the headaches, and I distracted myself with other interesting and enjoyable pursuits.

Here's another question: Why was I practically never self-deprecating? Maybe self-downing was *too* intolerable for me to tolerate—so I worked very hard to rid myself of it by somehow anticipating my later REBT solution of unconditional self-acceptance (USA). Or maybe I was born to be less of an over-generalizer than most people and naturally avoided what Alfred Korzybski called the *is* of identity: the huge mistake believing "I *am* what I do." Maybe—very likely—I was both.

Now the interesting thing is that I seemed to have been born—as well as raised—anxious. As a child, I *had* to succeed in important things—school, sports, public speaking, et al.—or else (1) I was pretty worthless and unlovable. Believing this was self-downing, which is what ego anxiety largely is. (2) Life was *awful. If* I did badly and was disapproved by significant others, I was "no good."

However, my "worthlessness" didn't include: (1) that I deserved severe punishment for being so "rotten"; (2) that God was going to put me into hell; (3) that other people were going to completely boycott me; (4) that I was worthless for feeling anxious and worthless; (5) that I was a completely incompetent person.

My anxiety, then, went with relatively minor feelings of self-deprecation: "If I fail at important tasks, I won't be as good or as loved as I *should* be. But I am not a thorough worm and no-goodnik. Not quite!"

My depression, when I had it about my disabilities, included little self-downing and no damnation for *being* depressed. And, as I said earlier, it didn't last. My low frustration tolerance was hardly abysmal. As the headaches went on for years I taught myself to live with them, continued my distracting activities, and probably became more achieving.

Oh, yes, speaking of achieving, I very much *liked* to do well at school, at writing, at regaling my friends, and at a few sports—Ping-Pong, handball, and walking. But I rarely rated *my self* as good, great, or glorious. I seemed to be a *natural* nondamner and nondeifier, even long before I read Korzybski and Bertrand Russell.

I was also not particularly hostile. To be sure, for a while I damned my physicians for the constant enemas they foisted on me. But usually I was a "nice" unangry child who intensely disliked people's *acts* but not the people. I forgave easily, and don't recall having any real enemies. Anti-Semites, tyrants, and other predators were "bad people," but I didn't obsess about them and merely, when I could, avoided them. My brother and I, in our joint fantasies before we went to sleep, had our sports and movie heroes—who, of course, liked us and hobnobbed with us. We hated their opponents—but not very vehemently. Mainly, my philosophy was live and let live.

3.

EARLY HOSPITALIZATION

My first hospitalization for nephritis was when I was five and a half. Up to my ninth year, I went to the hospital nine times, once for double pneumonia and the other times for nephritis. These visits were quite restricting—but only, usually, for a few weeks.

Other than my headaches—which occurred when I was home, too—my ailments were not very painful. Nephritis *silently* attacked my kidneys. I had edema (swelling) and frequent urination (a nuisance when lying in bed), but not much else. These symptoms even had some benefits. For example, in the children's ward, I had several friends and acquaintances. At seven, I fell in love with a Catholic girl. Always, I had several pretty nurses to love, lust after, and marry in my dreams. I had several attractive girls to think about sexually. Marvelous! No radio or television existed in those days, but I had plenty of books from the hospital library. No, it wasn't too bad. In fact, it was pleasant, but just not physically active enough. My mental activities blasted on.

When I was seven, however, I had my worst case of nephritis, with swollen feet, legs, and finally stomach, and I was hospitalized for ten long months. I especially missed school, my neighborhood friends, and my brother. I saw my mother only once a week at most, and virtually never saw my father. It was quite a stay!

The most dramatic event that occurred in my ten months' stay in the hospital was the tapping of my stomach. It swelled more than ever before, and the doctors decided to tap it with a needle, let the accumulated fluid out, and then let me go on my merry (or not so merry) way. But, unlike what happened during my tonsillectomy, they were *not* going to put me out with ether, and instead they were going to let me *consciously* have my experience. Well.

They said there would be no pain, and they were correct. They numbed my stomach, inserted a big needle in it (right before my eyes), attached a long rubber tube to the needle, and whaled away. Some fun! Into the needle and the tube flowed some of my vital fluids—a warm, milky fluid that went through the tube and into a bucket on the floor. It kept flowing out of my stomach into the damned bucket.

Well, they were right. There was no pain—and it was interesting to watch. I wouldn't have believed it. After five minutes the flow stopped, they patched up my stomach, and there I was—much less bloated.

I was also much less anxious. I really hadn't catastrophized before the operation; I almost enjoyed watching the flow; I liked the doctors' and the nurses' attention; the whole operation was much easier than the hellish enemas; and there I was, practically cured of my nephritis. In fact, a few weeks later, they let me out of the hospital.

Why didn't I catastrophize, when many children would have so indulged? I certainly often enough thought of grim things when, for example, I had chicken pox, itched like hell, and fantasized that it might grow worse, and I might even die. But I sort of *prophylactically* thought of disasters that could occur, met the enemy, sometimes saw myself dead, and then went back to the old living stand. So I died. Well, someday I'd have to, anyway, and that would be the end of all pain. No heaven, or anything like that. But no more pain. Done!

Naturally, I hated pain—like the enema pain. But, having seen one of my friends laid out in his coffin when I was six and he was seven, I saw how peaceful he looked and made that into a lesson. I was sad about his loss; but he, I decided, would be sad or pained no more. I therefore took all my imagined catastrophes to their bitter end—then calmly dropped them. The *end* (to me and to trouble).

So I half-believed my stomach incision would work out well—but if it didn't, I would forever lie peacefully at rest. No more hassles. Nothing.

Unfortunately, I didn't take that well to another ongoing problem during my ten-month hospital stay: constant blood-letting. This routine, I think, was applied mainly to me and not to the other children in the ward. For some reason, they took blood from my arm two or three times a week and took it from the other children every one or two weeks. This, of course, was unfair, but I didn't consider it so, because I realized that my medical condition seemed to "fairly" call for it.

It wasn't usually all that painful, because I have visible veins and they easily stuck the needle into one of them, although not always! Some nurses botched up the needle entry and had to try again—and again. There's no knowing in advance. So I feared having a botched and painful entry, and wanted to eliminate having one. How did I do this? In no way, except by calming myself down and hoping for the best.

I wasn't always successful, however. I feared the bloodletting cart approaching my bed and looked for it too often. Sometimes it didn't come. Good. Often it did come. Grr! For ten months it regularly kept coming. It took many of those months for me to conclude, first, that the nurse seldom botched it. Second, it wasn't *that* painful even if she did botch it. Third, I obviously had survived the bloodletting many times. Fourth, it really *was* for my general good. Fifth, I couldn't avoid it.

These last two conclusions finally sank in, and then I was less fearful. Also, there seemed to be less botching because of my reduced anxiety. So I finally got close to Reinhold Niebuhr's serenity prayer and accepted what I couldn't change. Maybe that experience helped me develop that philosophy for the rest of my life. I think I sort of started my therapeutic career at that time too—by talking to other children who feared painful procedures, and helping them to accept (without liking) them.

The other physical problem that started with my ten-month hospitalization stay was sleeplessness. None of the other twenty children in my ward seemed to be as afflicted quite as I.

I rarely go to sleep fast and easily—possibly because of the reasons I've already given. I am active and my mind is active—it doesn't *want* to sleep. I could say that life is too interesting to spend it sleeping. Too many problems—good problems as well as bad—practically cry out for solving. Then there is the problem of sleeping itself.

As I have already noted, I could easily live without sleep—if my body could. But, alas, it can't. If I sleep little, I am tired and not well functioning the next day. I realize that, so I am healthily concerned about my getting to sleep. Not immediately, but after an hour or two of pleasant wakefulness, I realize that I have a sleeping problem.

Ironically, having a sleep problem keeps me from sleeping. Thinking about how to get to sleep doesn't help me doze off, even when it's healthy problem solving.

As I soon discovered when bedtime arrived on the children's ward—at 8 PM, as I recall—and all lights (except dim general ones) were extinguished. I was wide awake, usually with interesting thoughts, including (after an hour or two) tactics for sleeping.

As many sages and psychotherapists have shown, you often can't win. If you are concerned about getting to sleep, you keep *looking* for a solution and trying out several. This method, of course, keeps you interested, alert, and awake. If you unhealthily worry about getting to sleep, then you keep watching the clock and predicting sleepless disaster. This method, of course, keeps you interested, alert, and awake. Drat it.

There's an old story that I often tell my worried clients. It's about a prince who could get permission to marry a princess only if he prevented himself from thinking of a pink elephant for twenty solid minutes. Naturally, he couldn't. For in telling himself, "I must not think of a pink elephant! I absolutely must not think of a pink elephant!" he kept thinking about one. Tough!

I didn't quite see this paradox at the age of seven, but I did clearly see that worrying about sleeping kept me awake. And, presumably, I couldn't *not* worry if I were to function well the next day. Double jeopardy! As I shall relate later, I beautifully solved my sleeping problem more than a half century later—and have for many years taught hundreds of other people to do so, too.

But at the age of seven, many things worked against me, including my own almost pathological activity and my definite pathological worry about sleeping. The old Presbyterian Hospital was on 68th Street, and the children's ward was on the second floor. Even with the windows of the ward closed (although they weren't closed in the summer, because there was no air-conditioning in those days), I could hear all the noisy traffic—including autos, trucks, buses, police cars, and garbage trucks, all night long, into early in the morning! Shit! My excellent hearing at that time (now, alas, gone) was an additional handicap.

I was also an excellent worrier. In those days, I was anxious about functioning well—achieving, solving problems, and being competent. Insufficient sleep equals insufficient functioning. I was well aware of that. Too aware, in fact. So I worried, worried, worried about getting to sleep and staying asleep. Worrying about *anything*, including sleeplessness, keeps me (and you) awake. Another paradox again!

As far as I can honestly recall, I never solved this sleep problem, and for ten months got—maybe—two hours of sleep every night. From that time on, perhaps because of that experience, I have been superbly conscious of time. I always have many things to do, like to get to them on time, and practically always do, partly by watching the clock.

I forgot to say that the children's ward had an old-fashioned Big Ben clock that chimed every hour. I thought it was stupid to have it and said so, but to no avail. So just about every night I would hear it ring at 1, 2, 3 AM and on. I would have definitely been aware of most of the hours by myself, without the clock's help. My awareness of time has distinct advantages—and disadvantages.

So I kept going—with very little sleep for ten months. Mind you, too, I did *not* take the daily two-hour nap that the other kids took. By the time 1 PM had arrived and I was supposed to nap, perversely enough, I was too awake to do so. My metabolism is high, and apparently I did not, as a child, need very much sleep. Two hours, usually, was enough.

I did, however, hit on a partial solution. About eight years later, I read a good book on insomnia that pointed out, among other things, that if you don't worry about sleeping or about anything else, but *peacefully* lie awake most of the night, your peaceful rest often is almost as good as sleep. At seven, before I read this book, I somehow agreed with it and spent most of every night peacefully unslumbering.

Did I merely relax or meditate and thereby pacify my resting? No, I discovered relaxation and meditation techniques in my twenties, and started to use them to good effect. I figured out from my experiences of being restlessly awake from 8 PM to 2 AM and then resigning myself to accepting the next few hours— from 2 AM to 7 AM—as sleepless, I could have *peaceful* rest. I put aside these five hours for *non*worrying alertness, said "What the hell!—use them as best I can!" and then did exactly that. I peacefully thought, fantasized, and solved problems, and beneficially *used* this waking time for my own individual purposes.

Oddly enough, my decision to *enjoyably use* five (or sometimes more) hours accomplished several things. It stopped my worrying about sleep and other problems. It distracted me from unenjoyable (and sometimes boring) pursuits. It was *pleasantly interesting.* I accepted me *with* my sleeping difficulties. It was not exactly a relaxation or meditation technique, but just as these methods give you something *non*destructive to think about, it also shunted aside my anxiety. Today, as I shall show later, I still use this peaceful enjoyment as well as relaxing methods. For in several ways, it *is* relaxing.

Much of my waking life in the hospital was also spent relaxing. I had good social relations with the other children, but also continually read—which I thoroughly enjoyed. I came out of my seventh year exceptionally well read, which I continued throughout my life. Maybe the "restricted" hospitalization led me to be much less restricted than the average individual. Intellectually, I grew and grew.

4.

SEPARATION ANXIETY IN THE HOSPITAL

Many children are prone to separation anxiety—especially when they first go to school and are separated all day from their home and parents. I treat children, and often their family members who can't take the whining child who absolutely refuses to be separated from (usually) mother and (occasionally) father. Children with severe separation anxiety, I find, also have other serious personality disorders—and I and REBT have a hell of a hard time ameliorating their separation panic. With persistence, we usually do.

My own separation anxiety was not that bad and actually lasted only the first day I was taken to kindergarten. My family was then living in Pittsburgh, which allowed early schooling. So my mother, afflicted with two other young brats, gladly hauled me off to kindergarten when I was four and a half.

I was confused the first day by the loss of my family and friends at home. The happy other children in my class seemed to thrive on being with the teacher and other children though far removed from home surroundings. I didn't realize that this was *after* they got acclimated to school and one another. So I rebelled, refused to listen to the teacher or do anything active, sat sullen in my seat, and wailed about being away from home. My mother almost agreed and was about to exit with me when the teacher calmly intervened and said she would handle it—that is, handle me. She practically tied me to my seat, ignored my wailing, and within an hour, I freed myself of my separation anxiety.

How? I saw that my mother had gone and would not return for several hours. I saw that the teacher was calm, adamant about my staying, and nice enough. I saw that the other kids happily ignored me or, in a few cases, were friendly. I saw that, no, I wasn't going to die.

So I quietly took all the "dangers" in, discounted their "horrors" when nothing bad actually happened, and lightly accepted what I couldn't change. I soon got bored doing nothing, while the rest of the class was happily participating in the pronunciation lesson the teacher was giving, and decided to stop my crap and stay. By the time my mother came for me—about three hours later—my panic was gone.

Though somewhat differently, separation anxiety erupted again during my ten-month stay in the hospital. Up to my fourth year, once I quickly got over my kindergarten separation anxiety, I don't remember any more of it except what I relayed above. But in my fifth year I fell madly in love with Ruthie, a blonde bombshell of my own age, was caught by our returning parents in what seemed to them a sex act (but was really only sex exploration), and was separated from her forever. I was desolate, as I report in the autobiography I am writing, for many months, but used my practical philosophy to live with this "horrible" adversity. After all, Ruthie wasn't the only bombshell in the world, and there would probably be others.

There was another one, when I was seven and in the hospital for a while. Gloria was two years older than I, had long black hair, and was a devout Catholic. Though we fell in love with each other almost immediately, I also knew that her Catholicism and my half-ass Judaism did not gel—at least in her parents' eyes. Marriage was forever, they held—but not with any Jewboy. I was not prejudiced religiously—many of my best friends were Catholics and Protestants—but Gloria's parents rigidly were. So I kept my big mouth shut about being Jewish, and we walked off into the blue together. And I kept fantasizing a Gloria-ous future.

My beloved wasn't as bright or as educated as I, but I became her mentor. That attached us even closer. It was as early as then that I discovered that girls had *real* problems, that discussing and helping them (rationally) with their problems tied them closer to me—and I used my discovery with good effect with Gloria. With my help, she became much less angry at her strict parents, junked her passive boyfriend, and kept pointing her prematurely growing tits in my direction. We were in separate but nearby beds, so we had nothing but a few toe-touching physical contacts. But that was enough! We sizzled together.

Our love of the century lasted for two months; but then Gloria was cured of her bronchitis and was about to leave the hospital. Alas! I wanted her to be well—but not out of the hospital. I was anxious before she was scheduled to leave and desolate afterward. I even finally confessed to her that I was Jewish and she forgave me for that and still was hot to run. But not her parents. They, when told that I was Jewish, wanted only to run—with her—away. And they did.

I soon saw—and hated—the hopelessness of our separation. In spite of our ecstatically promising to keep in touch with each other—and, of course, eventually marry, several incontrovertible blocks stood in our way: (1) Gloria lived in Brooklyn, I lived miles away in the Bronx. (2) She had no phone or friends with phones. (3) In the hospital, I too was phoneless. (4) She was "much" older than I—two damned years. Her parents held that girls should go with only older boys. (5) She was very strictly restricted by her rigid (and Catholic) parents. (6) She adored loud, raucous music and I doted on ballads and the classics. (7) She had trouble reading and therefore practically never read. (8) Gloria's parents even censored her mail. (9) When oh when was I to be unconfined from the hospital? (10) Etc.

Our separation at first killed me. I hated Gloria's tyrannical parents. I couldn't stand her refusing to rebel against them. I raved against the horrid unfairness of our being kept apart. I was anxious that my own plotting and scheming to see Gloria again would never be fulfilled.

Without consciously planning, I got over my separation anxiety and near depression. Nine months later, when I was back in school, I fell madly in love with a sexy-looking, very bright redhead. *That* was a relief. No more desperate thoughts about Gloria.

I also *worked* my way out of my obsession with being separated from Gloria. I kept using on myself the same "rational" arguments that I used with Gloria when she was angry at her dictatorial parents and overly passive boyfriend:

"Frustration of my desire is inevitable. No one gets everything he wants!" "Too bad I suffer from separation with Gloria. But it could be worse!" "Other girls will come my way and *some* of them will be as good as Gloria." "Even if they aren't, I can still enjoy our relationship." "Back to my reading. *That* never deserts me!" "I can still enjoy thinking about Gloria and my feelings for her from afar."

Notice that these are not elegant or thorough-going functions for my painful separation from Gloria. They never quite tackle my *dire need* for her or some reasonable substitute for her. They don't include REBT's antimusturbational philosophies, though they get somewhat close.

Anyway, these arguments—plus the redhead!—worked. I didn't entirely get over my loss—but I did undermine my irrational thoughts and feelings about the loss. Good. And it encouraged my future dealings with loss and undeserved restrictions.

5.

COPING WITH ABYSMAL PARENTAL NEGLECT

Although my mother and father seemed to love me, especially before I had siblings, I have long realized that I was a half-orphan. My parents were practically never physically (or sexually) abusive—not to me, nor even to my highly rebellious and obnoxious brother. They yelled at him a little—then (wisely) gave up on that tactic. So the little scoundrel got away with his obnoxious behavior.

My sister, Janet, was a depressed pain in the ass all her life; and she bothered my parents with constant whining. If anything, they favored her a little because of her whining, but mainly were unempathic and neglectful of her, too.

How come? For various reasons. First of all, my father, a traveling salesman when we were toddlers, was frequently away from home for weeks or months on end. When he was living with us, he was so busy with his daytime business activities and his nighttime pinochle games (or running around with attractive women, or whatever the hell else he did) that my younger brother and sister and I literally spent about five minutes a day with him (kissing him good-bye in the morning, just before we scooted off to school). Saturday and Sunday were again (as far as I could tell) mainly card-playing days for him, and only occasionally did he take an hour or two drive with us, in our chauffeur-driven electric Cadillac. When he finally was divorced from my mother when I was twelve (my brother was ten, and my sister eight), he was so devoted to our welfare that he came around to visit us literally less than once a year—even though most of the time he lived only a few miles away in Manhattan, while we were being raised on the streets of the Bronx.

As for my nice Jewish mother, a hell of a lot of help she was! Born at least twenty years before her time, thrown out of school in the sixth grade for compulsive talking, and quite unequipped to deal adequately with either marriage or parenting, she was much more immersed in her own pleasures and her own ego-aggrandizing activities than she was in understanding and taking care of her children. Her typical day: she arose about eight forty-five (after her eight-year-old son, Albert, had already awakened himself with the alarm clock, dressed, made his own breakfast, and proceeded to walk to school after crossing three of the busiest and most dangerous streets in the Bronx). She sloppily and desultorily did a minimum of cleaning, shopping, and child-tending. She spent most afternoons at her Temple Sisterhood functions or playing bridge or mah-jongg with some of her friends. She returned home between five and six o'clock (long after her son, Albert, had come home from school, made himself a snack, and helped take care of his younger brother and sister). She cooked or brought from the delicatessen very simple, ill-prepared meals that required a minimum of effort to get together. And she spent most nights with her friends (most of them fifteen or more years younger than she and from a lower socioeconomic strata), quite unrelated to her children (and often out of the house, leaving them unattended, in the charge of Albert).

Oh, yes: one more important thing. An additional affliction that I had to cope with during my various hospital stays—and particularly when I was hospitalized for ten months in a row— was that of separation anxiety. Up to my fourth year, I never recall being away from my mother, except for a couple of days at a time when she went to the hospital herself to bear my brother and my sister. And in each of these cases, I believed that she would return in short order, and I managed to go about my daily business quite well without her. I think I stayed over with friends of the family—such as my beloved godmother—during such times, and I don't remember resenting this or recall wailing and crying about my "lost" mother. When she did return home, I was genuinely delighted to see her again (and not in any way jealous, as I recall, of my new brother or my new sister). All told, I took the separation quite well. As for my father's being away at work and on business trips, as he frequently was, I easily adapted and didn't make any fuss about it. I got used to it, and in some ways, because of his lack of monitoring and imposing restrictions, I liked it.

When I went to the hospital for ten months, my mother at

first visited me every permitted day, during the regular visiting hours (which I think were on Sunday afternoons and between seven and eight o'clock Wednesday evenings). Occasionally, my father accompanied her, which was both unusual and good, as he rarely spent much time with his children; and if he ever talked or played with us (except briefly at some of our meals), I don't remember it. So when I was lying in the hospital, trying to get used to this new and greatly changed style of life, and both my mother and father came to cheer me up, brought me little gifts, and told me how they were proud of the fact that I was taking my stay so nicely, I thought that was great and looked forward to their visiting again soon.

These frequent visits quickly stopped, especially during my long stay in the hospital. My father practically never visited me during those times, and my mother, busy as she was with two younger children and a whole household to take care of, came irregularly. Her main visiting time would be on Sunday afternoons (from three to five, I believe) and she would usually be there at that time. But during Wednesday nighttime visiting hours, when most of the other children had their parents or others to visit and talk animatedly with them, no one showed up to see me. And during the summer, when my mother, brother, and sister went away for two or three months to Wildwood, New Jersey, my mother could not easily take the seven-hour round-trip train ride between Wildwood and New York, so she came to see me only about once a month.

So there I was, deprived of the Wednesday night visits that the other children on my ward received from their parents and others, and sometimes deprived of even a once-a-week Sunday visit. You can imagine how, when I first started to undergo this deprivation, I felt bad about seeing most of the other children's parents (and friends) regularly arrive and tend to them, while I had practically no one to talk to. My hospital friends were busy talking to their visitors, only a few of whom even bothered to talk to me, too.

That was really a wry time. I usually knew that my mother wasn't coming but I was not entirely sure, since she always told me, when she left on Sunday, that she might possibly drop in on one of the Wednesday evenings. So I always hoped against hope, when she didn't come, that she actually would surprise me and show up. But this rarely occurred. So I lay in my bed, reading or occupying myself in some other way, and trying to convince myself that it wasn't so bad that my peers had so many relatives and friends who kept coming to see them, while I almost exclusively had my mother (since virtually all my relatives on both sides of the family were in Philadelphia), and even then she didn't show up that much.

I did manage to convince myself that it wasn't that bad. Usually. I showed myself that I wouldn't have wanted most of the other children's visitors, anyway—as they were often noisy, stupid, and not understanding of children and their ways. I even convinced myself, and rightly so, that my own mother wasn't the best visitor in the world—since she too could be noisy, impossibly chatty, and self-centered in her own inimitable way—and I told myself that when she didn't come to see me I really wasn't losing that much. I also told myself that just because I was sorely afflicted with nephritis, and had to keep going back to the hospital, that in itself did not make the world owe me delightful visitors, and that pitying myself for not having them was not a very sensible thing for me to do. I finally convinced myself that although being by myself for an hour on a visiting day was not the greatest joy in the world—for I was quite sociable during my hospital stays and did a good deal of conversing with the other children and the nurses and doctors—it wasn't completely terrible and awful. It was just too damned bad—but that's the way it was, unfortunate. Thus, I anticipatorily invented part of REBT for myself before I actually created it almost thirty-five years later.

Of all the things I did to ward off misery during my childhood and to cope with the difficulties that life unceremoniously kept thrusting on me, I think that my handling this parental separation, with its accompanying feeling of rejection and loneliness, was about the most rational method I employed. As noted, in some ways it was a real precursor of REBT. For where I largely used, as shown in my handling of my stomach-tapping procedure, the techniques of cognitive distraction, in regard to my loneliness and lack of visitation, I mainly used the REBT technique of Disputing Irrational Beliefs.

This is the most elegant, I believe, of all REBT methods; and, to show you how prejudiced I really am, I find it probably the most elegant of all the many psychotherapeutic techniques that have ever been invented. Many other methods—even some of those used in psychoanalysis—to some degree help people with disturbances. But the deepest, most pervasive, longest-lasting, and most far-reaching of these techniques is Disputing (D) the Irrational Beliefs (IBs) that people use to create their poor Consequences (C), their dysfunctional feelings and behaviors.

To show what Disputing consists of, let me use the illustration of my not being visited in the hospital. The ABCs of

REBT in connection with this lack of visitation may be outlined as follows:

G (Goal): My desire to have regular visits by my parents.

A (Activating Experience or Adversity): My mother (and father) visited me relatively rarely when I was in the hospital, while most of the other children's parents (and friends) visited them twice a week.

RBs (Rational Beliefs): "I don't like this! I wish that my parents would visit me more and that I would have other visitors, too. How frustrating! But it won't kill me."

HCs (Healthy Consequences): Feelings of sorrow, disappointment, frustration, and annoyance. Action—if possible—to arrange for more visitation by my parents and others.

IBs (Irrational Beliefs): "This state of affairs *must* not exist! My parents *absolutely should* visit me more often—and even arrange to have other friends or relatives visit me, too. Isn't it *awful* that they're not doing as they should! I *can't bear* it! My parents *ought* to be damned and punished for this crummy behavior and forced to visit me more often. Poor me!"

UCs (Unhealthy Consequences): Feelings of anger and depression. Action of possibly telling my parents what bastards they are and letting the world know how horrible they are.

Assuming that these ABCs of REBT are correct—and I can assure you that tens of thousands of therapy sessions and many psychotherapy experiments have now shown me that they probably are—many steps can be taken to help people keep their Rational Beliefs (RBs) and surrender their Irrational Beliefs (IBs) (at point B) or to distract them from these IBs and thereby help themselves feel and act much better. Probably the best or more elegant of these techniques, however, is to help them actively and forcefully Dispute (at point D) their self-defeating ideas, and thereby not only give them up temporarily but ultimately basically disbelieve them.

What I essentially did to deal with my unhealthy feelings of anger and depression when other people were happily enjoying visits from their friends and relatives, and I sometimes uniquely in the whole ward was actually "enjoying" my loneliness, was to use the empirical and logical method of science (which REBT specializes in teaching people how to use) and to actively Dispute (at D) my Irrational Beliefs along these lines:

Disputing: "Why *must* this dismal state of affairs not exist? Why *must* I have as many friendly visitors as the other children on the ward generally have?"

Answer: "There is no reason why this dismal state of affairs *must not* exist. It if exists, then it has to exist—and that's the main way it can be: rotten! Nor is there any reason why I must have as many friendly visitors as the other children on the ward generally have. It would be lovely if I did; but just because such a state of affairs would be great and charming, that never means that it *must* exist. If my having more visitors *had to be*, it *would be*; and since it isn't that way, this clearly proves that it *doesn't* have to exist. [Too bad!]"

Disputing: "Where is it written that my parents *absolutely should* visit me more often—and even arrange to have other friends or relatives visit me, too?"

Answer: "It's written only in my crazy head! Obviously no law of the universe commands that they should do what I would like them to do; otherwise, they'd have to follow this law. Clearly, they're not following it. Therefore, the law is a myth!"

Disputing: "Prove that it's *awful* that my parents are not doing as they theoretically should."

Answer: "I can't prove that. It's certainly inconvenient—a real hassle! I'll definitely never like being by myself, when the other children on the ward are so nicely enjoying themselves with their visitors. So I won't! Why do I *have to*? Why *must* I be free of hassles and inconveniences? There's no damned reason why I must be. Sure, it's bad, quite bad that I am deprived like this. But if it were *awful* it would be totally bad—which it never is, as it could always be worse. Moreover, if I really mean that it's *awful*, I will view it as so bad that it *must not* exist. Which, of course, it does. Even if it is 99 percent bad—which, clearly, it isn't, because I can fairly easily survive my loneliness for an hour or two twice a week—it would never be 100 percent bad. Nor would it be *so* bad that it *absolutely must not* exist. So it never is *awful*—only a real bother."

Disputing: "Is it really true that I *can't bear* having considerably fewer visitors than the other children usually have?"

Answer: "Of course it isn't! If I really couldn't bear it, I would die of this kind of deprivation; which I haven't quite done yet! Or, even if I wouldn't die, I couldn't be happy *at all* if I were in a truly *unbearable* state. Well, *can* I have some degree of happiness, even when I am deprived of visitors? Naturally I can. I can read; I can think my own thoughts; I can at times talk to other children's visitors; I can do lots of things to enjoy myself, even if I can't do exactly the thing that the other children, with their visitors and their gifts from these visitors, are doing. So I'd better do some of these enjoyable things and stop whining about my not being able to *bear* this kind of deprivation."

Disputing: "Ought my parents really be damned and punished for this crummy behavior of often leaving me without visitors?"

Answer: "How ridiculous! First of all, their behavior is really not that crummy. My father is very busy in New York and often away on out-of-town business trips and couldn't possibly get in very often to see me; and my mother, what with two young children to take care of and all the other things she has to do, may be a bit neglectful of me, but her behavior is hardly *that* bad. After all, I'm not the *only* one she has to be concerned about; she does have *other* important things to do. If she had more time, she would most probably come more often. And when she does come, she is obviously happy to see me, brings me things I want, and treats me very well. So how is her behavior so crummy?

"Besides, let's even suppose that she's neglectful and that she could see me more often and simply refuses to go to the trouble of doing so. Even if she is acting in that wrong manner, how does that make her a *rotten bitch* or a *crummy person*? It clearly doesn't, since she does many other things very well and very lovingly. So, at the very worst, she is a person who acts badly (at least in *my* view) in this particular way. And although I may perhaps conclude that her deeds—or some of them—are rotten, I cannot justifiably conclude that *she* is rotten and that she should be damned and punished. After all, she's only human, and all humans are distinctly fallible. She's not *sub*human, nor is any person. And, like all humans, *she's* never truly damnable, no matter how bad some of her *acts* are. As for her being forced, in some manner, to treat me better, that's ridiculous. She has a right to whatever she does—including even the wrong things she does. And to force her to do the correct thing—or the thing that I really want—would be to take away her freedom. I certainly wouldn't want *my* freedom taken away like that, nor *my* being forced only to do the so-called *right* things. So why should anyone force her to be angelic?"

If I had used REBT to actively and thoroughly Dispute my Irrational Beliefs about my loss of visits when I was hospitalized, I would have done so along the above lines; and I would have most probably changed these IBs and ended up with Effective New Philosophies (Es) or rationally revised attitudes, which would have gone something like this:

E (Effective New Philosophy): "It's definitely sad and de-
plorable when I have few visitors, while the other children
in the ward have a good many who come to see them
almost every visiting day. But that's the way it is—too
damned bad. Life often is unfair and full of difficulties. But
I can surely bear, though I'll never like, those hassles. Even
injustice has its good points, because it gives me the challenge of being as happy as I can be in an unfair world. If I
could change this situation, I would; but since there seems
to be no way of doing so, I might as well gracefully lump
what I don't like and keep figuring out how to enjoy myself
even when I have no visitors."

If I truly arrived at these Effective New Philosophies and
kept going over them until I strongly believed them, I would
then experience the emotional Effects (of feeling healthily
sad, regretful, frustrated). And since I would not dwell on
these feelings (or the Rational Beliefs that produced them), I
would experience them only from time to time, rather than
continually. I would also, simultaneously, tend to bring on
the behavioral Effects of *acting* on my Effective New Philosophies and would do things like find enjoyable pursuits during
visiting hours, see if I could sometimes turn the other children's visitors into my own friends, visit with some of the
children on the ward who had no company that day, and do
other pleasant things.

Being only seven at that time, and not yet having fully
developed the principles and practice of REBT, I didn't do my
Disputing (at point D) as well as I would tend to do it today.
But I did perform it in a rudimentary manner, and I did arrive

at an Effective New Philosophy that approximated my later rational-emotive-behavioral views.

My goal, when I was a young child, was essentially the same as it has been during the ensuing years: to use my head to govern my feelings, but to govern them in such a way that I did not totally squelch them or arrive at Pollyannaish feelings of simulated joy. I wanted to retain *some* bad feelings, so that they would motivate me to keep trying to change the obnoxious events in my life and to activate myself to savor the present and the future. So I invented—though I did not realize it at that time—the REBT distinction between healthy negative feelings (such as sadness, displeasure, and irritation) and unhealthy negative feelings (such as depression, panic, and self-pity).

A good many years later, when I started doing REBT with my clients, I distinctly saw that many of my clients eliminated their baneful feelings (such as despair) by replacing them with equally or more hurtful emotions (such as flatness or intense rage). I realized that they were throwing out the baby with the bathwater, and that they had more, and much better, emotional choices than they were taking. Without having practiced an incipient form of REBT on myself for many years before this, I might never have realized how self-defeating my clients were, and I might have helped lead them up the same kinds of emotional garden paths that so many other psychotherapists have often done and still do.

I also see, today, that there are no clear-cut or perfect answers to our choice of healthy and unhealthy feelings to promote when we are struck by real Adversities. First of all, there are no *real* or *indubitable* calamities for all of us all of the time. Some of us—albeit few—actually *enjoy*, are *strengthened by, grow, and develop* from tragedies such as floods, hurricanes, cancer, AIDS, and even death. Severely physically and/or emotionally disabled people may *sometimes* be better off when they die. *Some.*

What about my advocacy of *healthy* feelings—such as sorrow, regret, frustration—instead of *unhealthy* negative feelings when you are sorely stricken with Adversity? For many years I was almost dogmatically sure that these emotions were much better achieved by my clients, readers, and listeners than their experiencing, under similar dismal circumstances, the *unhealthy* feelings of panic, depression, and rage. I am still *reasonably* sure that this is a better choice. But not *always* for *all* people.

I now, with increasing frequency, see that "bad" things are not *all* bad, nor "good" things all good. Yes, often, probably, under usual conditions, they are. Intense sadness—say, about the death of your child—is neither the same as nor as bad as deep depression. But it is bad enough! And depression about your child's death may propel you to actions that will help you help other parents, or the children of other people, to survive longer.

Just about everything, REBT holds, has both advantages and disadvantages. Devastating terrorism and war may, alas, be the main horror that finally drives us toward universal peace. And even universal peace, if ever achieved, may encourage inertia, purposelessness, and increased low frustration tolerance. Yes—really! Look at ancient and modern history for examples.

So I keep searching for and rooting out my dogmatism about "indubitably" good and bad thoughts, feelings, and actions. I only vaguely and rarely—when practically driven to do so—did this when I was an afflicted child. As an aging fol-lower of REBT, I do so much more.

From this material about my neglectful parents, I illustrate how I dealt with their absence during my ten-month hospital-ization pretty well. Not *elegantly* well, but well enough. I could have been very depressed about my neglect and loneliness. Maybe, briefly, I was. Once again, however, I accepted, without liking, the inevitable. First, I saw its (present) inevitability. Second, I saw that not I, nor anyone besides my parents, could *do* anything to change it. Third, I made myself feel *healthfully* sorry and disappointed, rather than *unhealthfully* depressed and angry. Pretty good coping mechanisms for a seven-year-old.

On some level, I was even more accepting. I realized that the future would bring me *more* lousy inevitabilities; and instead of hopelessly whining to myself (and others) about that, I started to *prepare* myself. I resolved to develop *greater* high frustration tolerance. Hell knows, I would need it!

My difficult childhood helped me become a stubborn and pronounced problem solver. If life, I said to myself, is going to be so damned rough and hassle-filled, what the devil can I do to live successfully and happily nevertheless? I soon found the answer: use my head! So I figured out how to become my nutty mother's favorite child, how to get along with both my brother and sister in spite of their continual warring with each other, and how to live fairly happily without giving up my shyness.

Does this mean that the difficulties I encountered *caused* me to become unusually rational during my childhood? Not that I can see. My sister had her own share of problems. She was the only female child; she had almost every existent man-ifestation of allergy (and a host of other physical afflictions);

she had closer contact with and was treated more inconsistently by my mother; she was somewhat persecuted by my brother; she was the youngest child and, although always bright, was not able to compete with her two unusually clever brothers; and she had various other handicaps. Why, then, didn't she, like me, develop more problem-solving skills?

My answer—following the longitudinal studies of Stella Chess, Alexander Thomas, and Herbert G. Birch—is that she was largely born with a whiny, demanding, injustice-collecting temperament and that consequently she *chose* to make the worst of her childhood conditions. Later on, as she entered the second half of her life, she worked very hard against her temperamental handicaps, chose a saner (though, significantly, religiously oriented) way of living, and began to be much happier. I, fortunately, was never quite *that* crazy; and in spite of my natural predisposition toward anxiety, shyness, and inhibition, I also had a biological tendency toward objectively perceiving, scientifically assessing, and often energetically correcting some of my irrational behavior.

Why? Sheer luck—and hard work.

6.

OTHER CHILDHOOD DIFFICULTIES

Expectedly, I had my share of other childhood difficulties, especially in my own family. My brother's rebelliousness and obstreperousness didn't bother me too much, because he fought against general and family rules—and not against me—until he was eight or nine. We were always close, especially in our joint nighttime fantasies. We went to sleep figuring how great we were and how all the sports champions and movie stars applauded our greatness. They had good taste!

In a few ways, Paul was a nuisance. Since I was a year ahead of him, was well behaved and a high achiever in school, his teachers kept calling me in to complain about him. "How come a bright boy like Paul keeps throwing spitballs in class? Why doesn't he do his homework? Doesn't your mother punish him for acting as badly as he does?"

I answered Paul's teachers as best I could, politely told them that he and my mother were not going to change, and refused to take responsibility for him and his delinquencies. But I found this questioning something of a nuisance that I, Paul, our mother, and his teachers never resolved. Oh, well.

Janet was a horse—or a filly—of a different color and I almost always had a difficult time with her. I was just about the only one who could stand her continual whining and fighting. Paul almost killed her a couple of times—knowing he might be exonerated "for getting rid of that impossible bitch!" I often acted as mediator, and at least stopped real bloodshed. My parents stood by and let the two of them fight.

It was Janet who always provoked things. Nothing, she said, was good in her life and everything—especially Paul— was bad. So she endlessly complained—and of course made things worse. She had her own share of problems.

Unlike Janet, I was also innately inclined to build some consummately clever defenses. My mother busied herself so much with avocational and entertainment pursuits that she left herself little time for overt self-hatred. My brother acted out many of his frustrations and hostilities—by refusing to do his homework, for example, and by sassing his teachers when they got after him about it—that he became a notorious rebel and achieved a villainous kind of acclaim. My sister whined so much about my mother's favoring "the boys" (a favoring that was almost completely a figment of her imagination since, by her whimpering, she actually managed to get most of the favors) that some people actually took pity on her. But I did even better: I did so well in my schoolwork, in being tractable and kind with practically everyone, in mastering the art of understanding others, in developing interesting hobbies (especially voracious reading), and in various other constructive pursuits that I could genuinely like myself for my accomplishments.

In other words, I built a whale of a lot of self-esteem. So what if I was fairly lousy at sports, in many aggressiveness pursuits, and in asserting myself with any of the girls with whom I was madly (and silently!) in love? So what if my brother and most of my close friends were better than I was in these respects? Who was better at English, math, history, and ten other subjects than I? Who would all my friends and classmates come to for practical advice? Who was more favored by practically every adult woman? Who best figured out (until, at the age of twelve, I became an unregenerate atheist) what God really wanted people to do to get in His good graces? And who best (albeit with a little backsliding) stuck to this kind of heaven-oriented conduct?

In sum, the conditions of my childhood were in many ways worse than those of most of my contemporaries. But I basically liked myself for the wrong reasons: I took these conditions as problems to be surmounted and I rather cleverly, and with deliberately arranged-for social approval, surmounted them. I based my worth as a human being—which I now realize is quite an error—on my achievements and my popularity; but I did such a good job of using this "wrong" method that I had a fairly happy, productive childhood.

I finally solved my problem with Janet when I was fifteen and she was still an inveterate bother. I had a hobby of collecting lyrics to popular songs, which I took down in shorthand from hearing radio renditions. She copied my hobby, but made a nuisance of herself by disarranging my originals and even discarding some of them. Preventively, with much irritation, I forbade her looking at them and hid them away from her. This induced her to hate me and complain more about everything being unfair and the "goddamned boys" being favored by our parents. Actually, I thought, she bitched so much that my mother and father usually favored her over Paul and me—to shut her up.

Anyway, I detested many of Janet's ways and rarely spoke to her. That at least quieted things down, but I knew something was wrong with my hatred. One Saturday afternoon, I saw a movie and was walking home when I thought over what happened in the movie. A husband and wife continually argued, finally got a divorce, battled over custody of their two children, and then the husband hired a thug to kill his ex-wife. That settled things!

But did it? Were her two children happy about the death of their mother? Were the ex-wife's parents better off? Was the clever police detective who pinned the killing on the husband and helped convict him pleased? Not exactly!

At fifteen, I was already a pacifist—thanks to reading H. G. Wells, Sinclair Lewis, and Bertrand Russell. So I deplored the violence in the film I saw and thought about some ways to stop it and make the world more peaceful.

Then the thought forcibly struck me: I was sometimes angry at Janet—and I would not exactly have liked to kill her myself (not me, pacifist!) but to cheer while someone else did the gory deed. I'd better honestly face that—and, right away, did. Boy, I was something of a thug, too.

Still on the way home, the obvious practical solution to my problem hit me—dammit, I would forgive Janet. I'd forgive her nastiness, anger, and depression—she was good at all three, whatever reasons she had for feeling them—and go one step farther and be nice to her. I'd stop upsetting myself with my own anger—and by showing it, of course, making things worse with her. That was the solution—forgiveness.

I didn't exactly invent the REBT answer to war and anger on my walk home from the movies when I was fifteen. I didn't arrive at the Taoist philosophy of accepting all living things, nor the Christian idea, "accept the sinner, but not the sin." Nor did I realize Alfred Adler's view of social interest, Martin Buber's valuing the I-thou relationship, nor Paul Tillich's existentialism and its unconditional other-acceptance (UOA). But I think I got close to their views.

Among other things, UOA stresses the practical side of social living: Since you *choose* to live with others—and certainly not as a hermit—and receive great benefits from doing so, it is only fair and proper that you strive for your own good—*and* that of other people. Moreover, as I have stressed for the last twenty years, nuclear, biological, and other weapons are becoming so available that it is only a matter of time before a few fanatical angry—and "totally just"—people are able to annihilate themselves and the rest of us. You'll see!

On a much smaller scale, I saw as I walked home from the movies that raging and having temper tantrums—as Paul and Janet steadily did with each other—harmed them, our parents, and even (moderately) me. I, too, though to a lesser degree, was being harmed by anger. My anger toward Janet, hers toward me, and our feelings and actions toward each other. How incredibly stupid! I didn't quite realize then all the pernicious results of anger—especially to the raging person. But I saw enough of its harm.

I immediately concocted a plan to erase most of my own anger toward Janet. I would go home and tell her that I was giving up all anger and damnation of others, especially her, even when I fully disagreed with their thoughts and actions.

In my walk home from the violent movie I figured out what to do about my hostility toward Janet, and I promptly went home and did it. I told her: "Look: I've sometimes been very mad at you for whatever reasons, and I now see that I was wrong. My anger only begets more anger from you and others and doesn't get me what I really want: your cooperation and consideration. I'm a pacifist, but I haven't been following my own philosophy very well. So I'm now trying to change and will work at doing so. Hereafter, I'd like you to tell me when you think I am angry at you, and I'll do my best to correct it and to treat you better.

"As an example, I've told you not to copy my song lyrics for the last few months, and I withdraw that. Hereafter, you have my permission to look at and use any of them—as well as my other materials. Just ask me for them—or even take them without asking—and they're yours. No exceptions!

"I'm not asking you for anything in return—except, again, to let me know when you think I'm angry at you. I'll try to work on that. But again, I'm not asking you to change or to do anything. You're free to do what you want."

I could see that Janet was deeply affected by what I said. She kept a shocked silence—but a pleasant one. She finally said, "I'm glad you feel that way. I've been angry at you, too. Maybe I'd better work on that."

She quickly did. She showed me where her own song lyrics were put away, and said that I could use them whenever I wished. From that day on, we weren't close friends, but our anger at each other, or at least our expression of it, decreased considerably.

Paul was very skeptical of my new approach to Janet. He saw its virtues but thought it would do little good. "She'll never change," he said. "She's a bitch!"

He was wrong. She changed toward me—and even toward him. They had fewer disagreements and fights thereafter, and he finally accepted Janet almost completely. Neither of us really liked her—for she remained depressed, often sullen, and close to no one in the family (nor, later, her own family). When he was thirty, her son, Joel, confided in me that he never could really relate to or converse with her. "She's into herself," he said. "She never really listens to me. So I shut up and largely avoid her. What's the use?" That reminded me that Janet was in that respect like our own mother, Hettie. Hettie was not exceptionally angry or mean, but she was almost always into herself. Joel was right.

My giving up my anger at Janet worked—for me and for her. For years before she died when she was in her seventies, she seemed to like me, confide in me, and took my advice to her quite well. She was still a depressive but, partly as a result of reading my books, accepted herself and others much more, and had a couple of boyfriends (after a nonamicable divorce from her husband, Norman) to whom she really related. I liked her improvement, but I can't honestly say that I liked her. She was okay—but not my cup of tea. Too bad.

Giving up my anger toward Janet distinctly helped me. As a pacifist, I accepted people in general, but not in particular. I often realistically appraised their distasteful acts, and unhostilely kept my distance from most of them. When I started to date young women in my early twenties, I got closer to them than I ever would have before, because I clearly saw their failings, including their lapses with me, but I accepted them *as persons* nonetheless. I frequently hated what they did—but not *them*, the *doers*. That characteristic led me to relate well to all my far-less-than-perfect girlfriends. So my practice in accepting Janet had many good effects.

Did this practice work with boys, too? Probably. I didn't really care too much about their inconsistencies or flaws—since I never intended to *live* with them, and never did. But I easily forgave them for their inconsiderateness—as I did with Janet. Fallible screwed-up humans they were—similar to Janet.

To this day—in my nineties—I am probably still critical of people's thinking, feeling, and acting. I have high standards of behavior—my own and others'—and realize people's lapses. I often—not too often!—try to help them correct their "bad" ways. But only for a few minutes do I upset myself about their "immoralities." Then, without rancor, I proceed to deal with them, with, apparently, little raises in my blood pressure (thanks partly to my experiences with Janet).

7.

HOW I STOPPED PROCRASTINATING

Procrastinating is almost the human condition—with some good reasons. At times, if you do things at the last minute, you will help yourself have clearer ideas and will be able to perform better. You will not get to it carelessly, too fast, and superficially. Sometimes.

The disadvantages of procrastination, however, are often enormous. You let projects pile up. You waste your time doing unimportant things. You let yourself be overwhelmed with too much to cover at the last minute. You do the project sloppily and leave out some important aspects. You bother other people who are expecting you to work faster. You often beat yourself mercilessly for your foolishly delaying.

Enough! In fact, more than enough! Knowing its hazards, and easily pushing them out of mind, I was born and reared a procrastinator. My mother was no slouch, but got much of her work done at the last minute—and rarely pushed me to do better. My father, though constantly busy, was not noted for promptness. And whenever we went with him for a (rare) outing, he was the last one in the car. When he awoke in the morning to greet us, he did so still lying in bed—and stayed there a half hour or so longer. He avoided taking responsibility for his three children and never pushed us to do anything promptly or well.

So I took it easy, did onerous things just before the deadline, and got by. Not exceptionally well, but well enough. Even in school, when I did unusually well with reading, I largely did my own chosen reading, and procrastinated on the school homework. When Michael S. Broder interviewed me when I was eighty-eight, part of our conversation went as follows:

AE: The other thing I do, which I started doing many years ago, is not to procrastinate. For example, I found out that when I wake up in the morning I'm usually tired because it takes me a few minutes to be fully awake. But I used to say, "I'll get five minutes more sleep." Because I had time, I realized I could sleep five minutes more. But then I'd sleep for ten or fifteen minutes. So I stopped that. When the alarm rings, I get out of bed immediately. No crap. I don't debate five minutes more, ten minutes more. When I was in high school I got away with murder because I was brighter than most students and I did my homework in the ten minutes between classes. So I'd get to the next class in two minutes and for the next few minutes I'd study the lesson for the day.

MSB: Then you wouldn't have to do it at home?

AE: Right. So I had my own rule. I never took a book home. We had a locker in school and all my books, especially the heavy ones, were in my locker. I had a notebook. But that was in the locker, too. So when I got home, and even on the train home, I read or talked with my friends. School was out and I wasn't going to bother with it until the next day. I got away with murder and I did pretty well scholastically. I think I came out something like seventh in my class of two hundred students, without my doing too much. Also, I didn't have to take practically any final exams because we had a rule in my school that if you were okay, had done your homework, and were getting along well in class, you didn't have to take the final. I had to take the Regents exam, like everybody else. But even there I figured out a system both in high school and in college of how much I had to study in order to pass the Regents to get a pretty good score. I majored in accounting in college. They gave us class manuals, so I just took two weeks at the end of the term to pretty well memorize the manual and I did very well. A's in accounting.

MSB: You know that's something you and I have in common. I was an accountant, too, before I became a psychologist.

AE: But I never practiced accounting because I found it boring. It was too easy. I had one or two jobs as a sort of bookkeeper, but I never really practiced accounting. What I did—because of my emphasis on saving time—was spend little time doing homework in high school. But when I got to college, during the first term I saw that was rather stupid because there was more work to be done. So the first term I sort of goofed [off] and I did all right. I got by, but not up to my level. And then the second term—oh, yeah, it was mainly the term papers, that's right—the term papers on major subjects, such as history or literature. We always had to do a term paper. So the first term I did them like everybody else did, during the last two or three weeks. But the library was crowded at that time so that wasn't a very good time to do it. So I decided against that. I think it was the second term—they gave us a term paper right at the beginning of the term. I picked my topics and I did my papers immediately, about four of them. Right away. My teachers were amazed, because nobody handed them in until after the term was practically over. So here it was two or three or four weeks into the term and I submitted my term paper. Because the library was uncrowded and I decided to get them over with so that I could coast the rest of the term. I didn't procrastinate like most people do—never get the paper in or get it in late—I always got it in ahead of time.

MSB: This efficiency is a very innate trait of yours.

AE: Yes. It's my thing. My mother wasn't that way because she did things lackadaisically. She was a rotten cook. She didn't make the effort; she cooked the food fast. My father was never around, so I never really knew him. I also became a nonperfectionist as a result of my nonprocrastination.

I write more than any other psychologist. When asked

how I could do so, I said that there were three main reasons. First, I have an electric typewriter and I know how to use it. I type fast and it has been a great help to me all my life. I learned in high school how to type. Second, at the time I was asked about this, in the 1950s, I didn't have a helpmate. That was a great advantage! I was in between women and didn't have a wife or lover, though I had been married before that. Third, I'm a nonperfectionist. When I write something, I could easily revise it and improve it. But, with little revision, I send it off to the printer and use the available time to write something else. It's mainly my nonperfectionism that lets me get things done because I finish them quickly. I don't continually revise them before they are published.

MSB: While you're on that particular subject, with all of the things you've written, it seems to me that your goal has always been when you get an idea to get it written down and then get rid of it and not worry about the format of it, how many copies you're going to sell, or any of those things.

AE: I try to do it well but not perfectly.

MSB: Not perfectly. But I mean also there's not a lot of emphasis on, for example, getting the best publisher. You'd rather get a publisher who's going to do it your way, then move on to the next thing. Is that accurate?

AE: The "best" publisher isn't often really the best. The trouble with publishers is that they may not push a good book.

One of my first books was *A Guide to Rational Living,* which was published by Prentice-Hall, one of the best publishers. Prentice-Hall never pushed *A Guide to Rational Living.* It sold well, but their editor, who was enthusiastic about it, left the company. So you can't trust the big publisher. That's why I had a lot of stuff published by Lyle Stuart and other smaller publishers. Some were pretty big, but some weren't. But, as you said, I get each book out as soon as possible and get it published even if it isn't the best publisher. Because you never know if the best publisher will really be good. I just had somebody recently tell me that she first went for the best publisher but then it brought out too many books so they didn't push hers.

I stopped most of my procrastinating when I was in my first year in college and sometimes went to the other extreme. I not only met my deadlines but easily beat them. As I began to publish more and more of my writing, I was increasingly asked to do articles and books. I would usually agree to such offers and then turn in my material a month or two early. I enjoyed getting projects done—and out of the way—and that also left plenty of time for revision and addition, for which the unkind editors frequently asked. And rightly!

The trouble is, I now sometimes take on too much. I do an incredible number of things, and nicely fit them into the hours I have available—individual and group-therapy client hours, workshops, talks, letters to answer, out-of-town presentations, etc. Most of these are scheduled in advance.

Some, alas, are unscheduled: e-mail and other questions about my practices and writings; old friends and trainees whom I haven't heard from in years; definitions of terms I use; donations to our nonprofit [Albert Ellis] Institute; requests for autobiography information; Web site presentations; requests to reprint some of my writings; arguments about my religious, political, and economic views; factual corrections of my written and spoken statements; and on and on and on!

I respond to practically all these requests as quickly—and as briefly—as possible. No farting around. Still they come! Being president of our Institute, a famous writer and speaker, a psychological authority, and a charismatic presenter has its drawbacks. If I don't watch it, I get overwhelmed with things to do and underwhelmed for time in which to do them. So I force myself to cut down on promising important articles, books, and lectures, and even radio and TV shows that would benefit REBT. Too bad! But there are still only twenty-four hours in the day and (especially with my older age) limited energies. Too damned limited—but not *awful*!

8.

COPING WITH FAILING, ESPECIALLY IN MY LOVE AFFAIRS

Except for physical prowess and strength, I have had a good record of achievement. Even physically, I have had *some* advantages, as in being a fast and inexhaustible walker (although not in my eighties and nineties).

I teach my clients (who listen!) that all of us often fail—and that is good. We learn largely by trial and error, providing that we abhor our *mistakes* but not our *selves* for making them. Most of the time most of us rate how well we achieve and then usually also rate *ourselves* as a good or a bad *person*.

This common human mistake—and it is a mistake—is a "logical" outcome of our being responsible for our achieving and our nonachieving. For we, the person, throw the ball well or badly—it hardly ever throws itself! Therefore we "logically" rate our poor *ball throwing* and "illogically" rate *ourselves* as a *poor ball-thrower* or as a "bad athlete" Overgeneralizing again!

I often have a hard time showing even my bright and educated clients that this kind of *self*-rating is illegitimate and harmful. Yes, we threw the ball badly and we were responsible for doing so. Even if we *irresponsibly* threw the ball badly—because, let us say, we stupidly drank too much before throwing it—we are responsible for our irresponsibility. We did it with our little hatchet!

So we can fairly accurately rate or evaluate our good (effective) or bad (ineffective) behaviors: choosing to play ball (okay); responsibly throwing the ball when it was thrown to us in the game (okay); irresponsibly getting intoxicated before the game (not okay); and throwing the ball poorly (not okay). Therefore, we conclude that since we made the right choices in deciding to play and the right choices of throwing the ball (both choices being responsible), and since we chose to get drunk before the game and chose to therefore throw the ball badly (both choices being irresponsible), we therefore acted irresponsibly and *are* irresponsible people.

False, even in this simple illustration. We *at times* act responsibly and *at times* irresponsibly. So we *are* not irresponsible (bad) people. To rate ourselves as bad people, we would have to show that we *consistently*, practically *always*, refuse to play ball, refuse to throw the ball back, when it is our turn to do so, deliberately get drunk before the game, and constantly throw the ball badly whenever it is our turn to throw it. This is very unlikely.

This means, fairly obviously, that no matter how responsible you are for a poor act, such as throwing the ball badly (meaning that you performed the act and even arranged to perform it badly), you cannot be globally rated as a *bad person*.

That also goes for your being responsible for (that is, you caused) poor behaviors. As Korzybski pointed out, the *is* of identity is false; you can't *be* what you *do*. A bad person would *always* and *only* behave badly—which of course no one does. Even mentally deficient and brain-injured people *sometimes* act well. And a good person would *always* and *only* behave well—which, again, no one really does.

Performance anxiety, which I had as a child and teenager, resulted, as it practically always does, from my musturbation. I *had* to be at the top or near the top of my rapid-advance class. I *needed* to speak well to my friends—and to new acquaintances. I *demanded* that I be good at several sports, especially handball and baseball. I wasn't crazy enough to think that I had to do *perfectly well* in all important activities. And I didn't insist that I needed to do well or else I was completely incompetent and worthless. My self-downing wasn't abysmal.

But I still felt that it was *awful* when I importantly failed and that it made me something of a *lesser or inferior person* (not quite a total shit—but close).

I was especially horrified about personal rejection. If somebody got higher class marks than I, was better at baseball, or told jokes better, I was unhappy. But I lived through it all and hardly thought of suicide. I think I told myself that they were better now, but that the next time I might well beat them out.

I was pretty good, too, when I failed to get accepted by other males. After all, I had a few close male friends but I hardly doted on them, and they were easily replaceable with other males. I never had a crush on or was madly infatuated with boys or men, with one exception. His name was Jimmy Gallagher, and he was my classmate for a few years.

Not only was Jimmy smart, but he was also unusually handsome and well built and was an outstanding athlete in several sports. Actually, I never got close to him, since he was far ahead of me in athletics, made every sports team imaginable while I made none, and he was so busy as a team leader that we hardly ever got together outside of class. Even when we played handball, which I was reasonably good at, he played only the very best players, so I rarely got together with him. But I envied his looks and his physical prowess, and though I was not madly in love with him, I did have something of a crush. I felt inadequate and at least moderately put myself down compared to him. But I was only moderately anxious when I occasionally spoke with him.

One day, I had an unusually good talk with Jimmy when we were on the way home from school, and I told him how much I admired him and in some ways would like to be like him. To my surprise, Jimmy said that he greatly admired me, especially as being brighter, much more widely read, and nicer and more considerate than he. I was pleasantly shocked to learn that my hero, Jimmy, envied me in several respects.

Naturally, I was pleased—and also relieved. I realized, during our talk and by thinking about it later, that if he had not rated me so highly, I would have put myself down. As we note in REBT, I would have thought that I had nothing to offer Jimmy—and was therefore something of a nothing myself. At the age of twelve, I compared myself to other "superior people"—like Jimmy. If I lacked desirable traits, especially physical ones, I honestly rated them as "inferior," and also rated myself, my essence, as "inferior."

Jimmy, in our talk, did me the favor of saying that in some

ways, I was "better" than he; and, in an instance, I then (foolishly!) thought that *I* had lost my "inferiority" and become "equal" to a "superior person." Saved from shithood!

I realized, as I was writing this estimation of my global "worth" when I was twelve, that like almost everyone, I suffered from "self-esteem"—what I later called "the greatest sickness known to humans." I sanely rated my important traits—mental and physical—as "good," "indifferent," or "bad," in accordance with cultural standards. But I also sometimes rated my "self" or "being" as "good" or "bad" by "unsane"—according to Korzybski—social standards.

Fortunately, I did not devalue myself strongly, rigidly, and persistently—as, of course, many people do. Living by a combination of innate, social, and self-created "personality" tendencies, I was a *light* victim of grandiosity and self-deprecation. Had Jimmy Gallagher put me down, I would probably have been somewhat depressed myself—but not intensely, as a good many of my clients are. I would have felt like a *half*-shit for a few weeks, and then got myself back to enjoying my "good" traits and my life.

That is what happened with me and several of the girls that I kept falling madly in love with from the age of five onward. *In-lovedness*, as differentiated from merely *loving* someone (or what H. G. Wells termed "loving kindness"), is obsessive-compulsive (at least in my case). When I am *in love* (with a person or a cause), I think of her (or it) steadily, compulsively. I *adore* her, lengthily ruminate about her, have glorious fantasies about her (and me), madly and unrealistically preoccupy myself with her and neglect other important aspects of my life.

In doing so, I again put my worth on the line—believe that I am a "better person" if my beloved values me and am a "lesser person" if she doesn't. I do not, however, *completely* or *prolongedly* believe that. I don't consider myself *totally* worthless or *unlovable*. And I depress myself only for a while if I get rejected by or otherwise lose my beloved.

This is what dramatically happened when I was five and unsanely in love with Ruthie, whom I described earlier as "a blonde bombshell." She was, as everyone including me seemed to agree, a five-year-old Marilyn Monroe type. She and her parents lived in an apartment house next door to ours on Bryant Avenue (in the East Bronx) and we doted on each other for several months. Then—as I tell elsewhere in grim detail—tragedy ensued.

Being left alone, when our parents all went to the theater on a Saturday night and our supervising maid wrongly took a nap, Ruthie and I kissed passionately, undressed each other, and then (bright idea!) I took a glass of milk and a funnel, and out of curiosity tried to pour some of the milk into Ruthie's vagina. Maybe I would have succeeded and discovered where her genital orifice finally went, but at that crucial moment our parents came home and found us animatedly "having sex"—which, actually, we weren't.

My parents bore up pretty (humorously) well, but Ruthie's were absolutely horrified. They whisked her home, almost immediately moved to another part of the city, and parted us forever. Forever!—with not even a final good-bye.

I knew that I was unforgivably wrong, because exploring Ruthie's vagina was *my* idea—though she, alas, fully consented. So I blamed my stupid action—and my total self—and was quite depressed for weeks. When I finally faced the fact that Ruthie and I would never go off together, I was very sad and regretful—but soon turned to my main hobby of learning to read and my other enjoyable childhood affairs. I diverted myself quite well from the (then) greatest tragedy of my life. This diversion started a pattern that lasted for several years.

So my self-rating for my deficiencies and mistakes was always there—but not in the worst form. The same was true with sports, too. I was always thin and frail; and, especially with my nephritis, I was forced to avoid rough sports like wrestling and football. I faced and acknowledged my physical deficiencies but compensated for them in mental ways. I partially withdrew without considering myself a thorough weakling and no-goodnik.

With my steadily falling in love, it was worse. I *passionately* wanted to be admired by my beloveds; and I was so afraid of being rejected—and of downing myself for my failing to gain reciprocal love—that I made myself utterly shy. Not with other males—with whom I got along well, especially if they were older and wiser. But, after I lost Ruthie, all my insensate passions were for years unrequited. Did I fail to win my beloveds? Not exactly. Much worse, I abysmally failed to *try* to win them. If I could help it, I shyly avoided talking to them, telling them how I felt about them, and even flirting with them with my eyes. I was *ashamed* of letting them see how I favored them— and of their not favoring me.

I was practically always madly in love with one (or two) of the "superior" girls in my class. I can remember that from six to twelve I was intensively in love with six girls (one each year!), one teacher, and Mary Pickford, Dorothy Gish, and several other movie stars. At being in love, I was no slouch!

However, until I was twelve and in junior high school, I never even flirted with one of these beauties. Letting them *see* I was mad for them was shameful and forbidden because they might not return my love—and I might see that! I believed I was not handsome enough to win them. I thought they might reject me for my physical frailness. I was ashamed of my (lusty!) sexual desires for them. You can imagine all the reasons I was inadequate for *this* marvelous girl, because I was self-downing!

Finally, at thirteen, I fell in love with Isabel, an exceptionally bright, attractive, and talented girl in my junior high school class—and dared to flirt with her across the room. She flirted back for a year! Both of us, I am sure, knew that we were born for each other, would marry, and have several beautiful and highly intelligent children. How did we know this? Not by smiling at each other—for we were too shy for that. Instead, we knew with shy but steady facial glances. But our shy looks, often repeated, told a million stories.

To make matters much worse, with Isabel I had a secondary symptom—shyness (self-downing) about my shyness. I knew I was stupidly scared of *openly* flirting with her—and of going miles further. I was painfully scared of being scared—not only scared of being rejected but panicked about my panic about being rejected. That, naturally, gave me *two* self-deprecating symptoms. So I never risked talking to Isabel—or even flirting with her again. I also knew that my fellow students might put me down for flirting, for not openly making overtures, and for getting rejected if I did make them. So although Isabel and I knew we were flirting, I think we were the *only* ones who knew.

Anyway, I did nothing (but surreptitiously flirt); I never

talked with Isabel, let her be transferred to another class and, finally, another school, and never discovered what she *really* felt about me. I was "sure" I knew; but I never truly knew. When we went to different high schools, and I never saw her (or tried to see her) again, I thought about her for the next several years and didn't replace her with a new passion. How idiotic! How idiotic for being so idiotic!

As ever, I survived alone—without real, truly depressive self-downing. Until I fell in love with Kathie, at the age of sixteen. She was not *as* attractive or bright as Isabel, but I and my brother, Paul, were very friendly with her for a summer we spent on vacation in Wildwood, New Jersey.

Kathie, something of a tomboy and very assertive, seemed ready to be more than friendly. But I never spoke about sex or love to her—although we did speak of everything else—because I was again afraid of rejection. If anything, she would have *nicely* rejected me. But by not "winning" her, *I* would have put myself down. So I never tried; and, again, I berated myself for not trying. What did I have to lose? Nothing but my own "self-esteem." So I stupidly held onto it.

I finally got over my ego anxiety about falling in love years later, when I was twenty-four. For more than a year, I fell in love with Karyl, another very attractive, bright, talented, young actress, nineteen years of age. Maybe I should have stayed celibate! Karyl was one of the most disturbed people I had ever known. As a psychologist, I would diagnose her as a woman with severe depression, borderline personality traits, and obsessive-compulsive. At the age of fifteen, she became so overtly depressed that she was seen by a psychiatrist who recommended that, because of her suicidal tendencies, she be allowed to quit school before the legal age of sixteen. He said that she was bright enough to not need further school. As is the case with many individuals with severe personality disorders, both her parents were chronically anxious, and her only brother committed suicide a few years after I met her, when he was only twenty-eight. Karyl was the by-product of partly bad heredity *and* partly poor environmental teaching.

The full story of my holocaust with Karyl, including my marriage and divorce from her only a year after our torrid affair started, will take a few autobiographical volumes. Here, in brief summary, is the worst of it.

At the age of nineteen, Karyl madly loved me—and a few other men. All her life she obsessively became violently—and I mean violently—infatuated with one or two men at a time. These men often included handsome "bums"—a term she described them as—who refused to work for a living, and who exploited women and others. Soon after I met her, she fell for Ronald, a thirty-five-year-old panhandler, left him for me, then left me (after our marriage!) for him. Then he left her for his former girlfriend, then Karyl became suicidal, then she went back with me again. What a story! Unbelievable. Finally, with my help and with the use of rational emotive behavior therapy, she became unusually sane and unaddictive in her seventies and was devoted mainly to her five children (by her husband, Tom) and to me and REBT.

Within a week of meeting Karyl, I was both frantically in love and sexually obsessed with her. I was technically a virgin, although by this time I had had numerous petting experiences with women I hardly knew and with whom I wasn't emotionally involved. But I was tempestuously involved with Karyl, and our sex play was obsessively exciting—and erratic.

To say the least, Karyl was exceptionally inconsistent in her love and sexual feelings for me. One day I was tops, and the next day she was into her own navel (and/or some other man's) and I was amatively and sexually neglected. To say that her sex and love feelings (and actions) toward me were volatile is putting it mildly.

Any man, I think, would have suffered from Karyl's mercurial behavior. On the one hand, I sensibly kept revolting—and honestly telling her—that I would leave her. But I compulsively kept hanging on and feeling depressed, anxious, and angry, although not every day. I periodically recultivated my sanity, gave her an ultimatum about leaving, and then still unsanely stayed.

I finally resolved my obsessive-compulsive, up-and-down passion for Karyl and have written about how I did it in my address, "The Evolution of Albert Ellis and Rational Emotive Behavior Therapy," which I gave to the Evolution of Psychotherapy Third Conference in Las Vegas in 1995. As I reported at that time, I was getting nowhere with Karyl when I loved her madly "because of her indecision about how much she loved me" in return. On the one hand, I wrote, she would say her love for me would put Juliet's passion for Romeo to shame. On the other hand, a few days later, she would say I was too esthetic for her, would show interest in other men, and would neglect me considerably. Several talks with her and thirty-page letters to her about her inconsistency got me and her nowhere. She rigidly stuck to her indecisiveness. I wrote some sixty-five years later:

One midnight, when I had spent a wonderfully conflicting evening with Karyl and was on my way home to my apartment in the Bronx, I was sorely troubled about our still see-sawing relationship and decided to go for a walk by the lake in [the] Bronx Botanical Gardens and to reconsider our on-and-off affair. In walking around the deserted lake, I thoughtfully decided that my love for Karyl was stupendous but that it had too much pain attached to it—especially when she continued her stark ambivalence. Maybe, I thought, I should quit the whole affair and find someone who would love me steadily instead of with startling intermittency.

Suddenly, I saw the way out of my—not to mention Karyl's—dilemma. It was not my strong *desire* for her that gave me so much trouble when it was not thoroughly fulfilled. No, it was my *dire need* for her love. I foolishly believed that she *absolutely had* to return my feelings in kind; and that and only that would solve our problem. Well, that was horseshit! I saw that I could, if I wished, keep my powerful desire, urge, and love for Karyl—and I could simultaneously give up my *need, demand,* and *insistence* that she feel exactly the same way as I did.

That was really an astonishing thought: I could love without needing! Indeed, I now started to see, all those other girls with whom I kept obsessively falling in love since the age of five, whom I couldn't get out of my mind, and whom I was terribly anxious about their loving me back, were in the same category as Karyl. I foolishly thought that I *needed* them—that I couldn't live happily *without them,* and *had to* cement a stupendous relationship with them forever, even though I was too damned shy to let any of them know my feelings.

Need, not love, was the issue! That, I saw as I went for my walk in the woods, was my and everyone else's real problem when we were anxious, depressed, and enraged. We needed—or foolishly *thought* we needed—something that we importantly wanted. We asininely insisted that we absolutely *must*, under all conditions and at all times, be loved, *should* get what we want, and ought *never* suffer serious frustration. What quaint ideas! How pernicious! How could we possibly be happy—really and persistently happy—when we rigidly held to these unrealistic notions? We couldn't.

So, believe it or not, in that one twenty-minute walk by the lake, I gave up most of my neediness—especially my dire need for Karyl's love. I still desired very much to be with her and would still try to win her love. But I definitely didn't *need* it. Just as soon as I could, I would tell her this, tell her that I had stopped insisting that she *had to* return my strong feelings, and then see what kind of a relationship, if any, we could work out. If, at worst, she wanted to break up, I could accept that. If she wanted to go on with the relationship and still be ambivalent, I would accept that, too. But, if so, I would eventually find another woman who would be more constant. Not that I *needed* to, but just that I *wanted* to find one.

I got together with Karyl the very next night, told her how I had propelled myself out of my need for her, and asked her what she wanted to do now. To my surprise, she was very impressed with my newly found nonneediness, wished that she could have it herself whenever she was madly in love, and suggested that we should have an experimental, nonneedy marriage. We would secretly marry—because we didn't yet have the income to live together—would maintain an open relationship, and would see how it all worked out. As long as we were both nonneedy, maybe it would. But it if didn't, too bad. Neither of us would have to feel hurt, angry, or depressed.

RATIONAL EMOTIVE BEHAVIOR THERAPY

How Karyl and I actually began and later ended our marriage is another story. The main point of this one is that I really did make a startling change in myself during my walk around the lake in the Bronx Botanical Gardens. For the rest of my life I have had very strong desires—many of them!—which I have striven to fulfill. But I have rarely thereafter thought that I *absolutely needed* what I wanted, nor *strongly needed* to avoid what I abhorred. And later I put antineediness, antiawfulizing, and antimusturbation solidly into REBT.

I did so in 1955, at the start of rational emotive behavior therapy. The dozen irrational beliefs that I originally postulated as a main source of human neurosis all include explicit or implicit musts and needs. Later on, after I had used REBT for a few years with hundreds of clients and had done a few research studies on it, I more clearly stated that when people are classically neurotic, they seem to have one, two, or three basic or core musts and needs: (1) "I *absolutely must* do well or I am no good!" (2) "You *decidedly must* treat me fairly and considerately, or you are a rotten person!" (3) "My life conditions *absolutely have to be* the way I want them to be, or I *can't stand it* and can't have any real happiness at all!" Many other irrational or self-defeating beliefs exist, as I and other cognitive-behavior therapists have pointed out. But underlying them and basic to them seem to be implicit or explicit musts, shoulds, demands, and commands. Whether I would have ever seen this so clearly without my getting over my own neediness during my walk around the lake in 1936, I'll never know. But that walk and the thinking I did in the course of it certainly helped!

Ironically, then, Karyl gave me some of the worst times in my life, and thereby practically *drove* me into my dire neediness about those times. Ironically, too, she helped me think of the essence of much human disturbance—neediness—and greatly benefited herself by my concept (and that of the Zen Buddhists and Karen Horney) many years after she helped me theorize about and act against it and put it in a central place of REBT. Karyl, in her later years, unneedfully kept attaching herself to me, and we had a fine friendship until she heroically died of emphysema and lung cancer in 2001.

Actually, the greatest passion of my life was with Gertrude for six years, when we ecstatically loved each other from 1942 (when I was twenty-eight and she twenty-five) to 1947. Again, Gertrude and my infatuation with her deserves, and will get, its own volume. Here let me briefly say how I coped with its difficulties.

Gertrude was a highly attractive blonde school teacher, a brilliant conversationalist, and an outstanding relater. I met her in 1942 through my oldest friend, Manny Birnbaum, who was her cousin. Within a week of dating, we were startlingly in love, although she had a "nebbish" of a husband in the army in Europe and I was just about to start my graduate studies in clinical psychology at Columbia University, was working full time to pay my tuition, was running the Love and Marriage Problems (LAMP) nonprofit institute, was already a (book-taught) authority on love and sex, and was writing politically. I especially was writing a multivolumed book, *The Case for Promiscuity*. Gertrude, intent on divorcing her husband soon after he was released from service in the army, was compulsively looking for her next husband.

She quickly chose me and I her, and we soon put all prior loves to shame. For six years—during which she divorced her husband—we saw each other practically every day (though she lived with her widowed mother), and we had great sex and few disagreements. Although by this time I was an accomplished and somewhat promiscuous lover, Gertrude taught me much about ecstatic sexuo-amative life—and I taught her a thing or two as well.

Everything went remarkably well until I got my PhD in clinical psychology in 1947 and the time to marry or not approached. We even looked for an apartment to live in—but that brought out our crucial domestic differences. For dating together, we were ideal; for domestic living, we were incompatible. I very much wanted an apartment with at least one solidly doored room, where I could be and work alone at times, and Gertrude wanted an open apartment with *no*—yes, no—solid doors. She was a *compulsive* relater. Worse—if possible—she wanted to give at least two dinners or parties every week at which she would invite several friends for her—and my—"edification." Two *every week*.

We parted company—or close relating—at that point and mutually decided against marrying and for her looking for another husband, which, in a few weeks, she found—and actually married.

I was exceptionally sad and, unusually, actually cried a little. The one thing that kept me from being depressed was the neediness I had given up in my walk around the lake in the Bronx Botanical Gardens when I was in love with Abysmally Erratic Karyl. I kept that lack of neediness and have never lost it since. I thought I would never again find a remarkably love-and-sex compatible partner like Gertrude; and I never have. But also, being an authority on love and sex, I knew that our romantic in-lovedness would fade after a while and that it had so far (five years!) lasted because, as Stendhal paradoxically observed at the beginning of the nineteenth century, we were not living under the same roof. While still being in love, I faced this reality. So, in her own way, did Gertrude, who was madly in love with permanent togetherness, with or without superromantic amour.

In my "Evolution of Psychotherapy" conference paper in 1995, I mentioned my avoidance of feelings of depression when my notable in-love relationship with Gertrude evolved into intense friendship and love when I was 33. I gave some impressions of myself and my disrupted passions. I wrote:

Although I seem to have been born and reared with a strong propensity to make myself anxious rather than depressed, I have some normal neurotic tendencies to depress myself when things are going unusually badly. Thus, I depressed myself for a while when I was thirty-three years of age and I broke up with Gertrude, whom I had passionately loved for six years, and still loved when we parted.

I felt depressed for a short while, but quickly started to use the methods I had previously used to overcome my feelings of anxiety, and was pleased to see that they worked very well. I strongly convinced myself that I didn't *need* to live with Gertrude, though I very much wanted to do so. I made myself see that she wasn't the only possible mate for me; that I could have a good life without her; that I wasn't a loser for not living up to her highly social standards; and that I would in all probability soon find a more suitable partner. That was pretty good, cognitively. But I also threw myself into more studying and writing; I started building my psychological practice; and I began actively dating, which soon led to my having another steady love relationship.

This experience tended to show me that feelings of depression, like those of severe anxiety, are usually related to demands that I (and other people) *absolutely must* perform well and *must not* be deprived of their important wants. Although I agree with Aaron Beck that specific automatic thoughts that people frequently use to make themselves anxious are somewhat different from those that they use to make themselves depressed, I still think that their underlying *musts* and *demands* are similar. Thus, I have said for years—and I still do—suppose that I, you, or anyone else thoroughly believes, "I *prefer* very much to do well and be loved by significant others, but I never, never *have to* fulfill these preferences. Too damned bad if I do not achieve them! I greatly *desire* to get what I want when I want it and to avoid severe pain and discomfort, but I never *need* what I desire and I can always find other enjoyable things. Tough shit if I am deprived! Now let me work like hell to try to get what I want!" If anyone really thinks this way and consistently carries these thoughts into action, would he or she ever become and remain severely anxious or depressed? Yes, perhaps, if their body chemistry was severely awry and they had endogenous anxiety or depression. Otherwise, I doubt it.

Anyway, my belief that both anxiety and depression usually stem from strong absolutistic musts, needs, and demands, and that they can mainly be relieved by thoroughly giving up these commands and changing them back into *only* the preferences from which they originate, this theory and practice of REBT once again largely stems from my own emotional growth and development. And my use of the main principles of REBT on myself, sometimes before I even formulated them for others, led, I think, to my own further growth and development.

For the most part, then, I very sadly, and not *depressively*, accepted Gertrude's and my decision to end our outstanding romantic attachment. We remained friends for over twenty years. In fact, we were sex-love friends after her marriage and she talked about her divorcing her husband and marrying me again until, a little later, he died in an unfortunate accident. We also considered marrying a couple of years later, when she suggested using her insurance money, from the death of her husband, to put me through medical school and psychiatric training. But we always wisely kept our domestic incompatibility in mind and refrained from matrimony. Gertrude led a tragic life with her next husband, who kept her under wraps and who committed suicide later. But we always kept in communication and never forgot our wild years of romantic love. Nearly sixty years later, when I have reached the age of ninety, I still fondly, and with some sadness, remember it. But with no guilt or depression. I am still not needy.

Let me end up with one more sad breakup, with Janet, with whom I lived for thirty-seven years, from 1965 to 2002. Janet, once again, filled my in-lovedness bill. When I met her in 1964 she was exceptionally bright, talented, and sexy, only twenty-four years of age to my fifty-one. We dated regularly for six months and then decided to live together at the Albert Ellis Institute's new building, where she first became the very capable office manager. She went back to school to finish her degree in sociology and then graduated with a PhD in clinical psychology from NYU. She later became executive director of the Albert Ellis Institute in New York.

I was clearly in love with Janet for a while. But, as Stendhal predicted, that didn't last when we began living together and was replaced by a loving relationship. Unlike me and

Gertrude, I was in some ways mutually compatible with Janet while living together. We were both busy most of the time—with managing the Institute, seeing individual and group therapy clients, giving talks and workshops in New York, writing letters and taking phone calls, and doing various other constructive work. Writing kept us busy, especially with my many books and articles, but Janet also published a number of articles and one book, *What to Do When He Has a Headache*. I had many friends, mainly by mail, and Janet had considerably more family and social relationships than I. We got along when we were together and when we were apart, since we gave each other considerable freedom—including sexual freedom. We disagreed about various things—but amicably.

Without much discussion, and with no fighting, Janet decided in 2002, after thirty-seven years, to quit her job as executive director of the Institute, and to set up her own apartment and psychological practice. In the main, from what she said to me, she felt that I was too preoccupied with professional activities, both at the Institute and with much traveling, and that I really didn't relate closely enough to her—as, especially, did her four nieces and her one one-year-old (and very cute!) nephew.

I was somewhat shocked at Janet's feelings, since I thought our relationship was imperfect but quite solid and good. I could easily live without ties to Janet's family—because, except for my brother, I was not close to my own family while they were living. But (after thirty-seven years) I really liked Janet and thought that she greatly contributed to my (and the Institute's) life. But I immediately took the separation from Janet well, continued to be quite friendly and helpful to her—particularly in some disagreements she had with some Institute personnel—and missed her and our partnership considerably. It was very sad to part when I was eighty-eight and could well use Janet's steady help as a full collaborator. My freedom became a little too free!

As usual, my lack of neediness saved me. From the time Janet left, to the time of my major intestinal surgery early in June 2003, I lived alone in my large (half-bare) apartment. It was far from ideal, but I bore it well. Since my surgery, which I write more about in a later chapter, I have nursing care around the clock. I am also greatly helped by my assistant and dearest friend, Debbie Joffe, with whom I enjoy an extremely close and loving connection.

9.

COPING WITH FAILING, ESPECIALLY AT WRITING

In some ways I am considered the most successful writer on psychology. To be sure, Wayne Dyer (with *Your Erroneous Zones*) and David Burns (with *Feeling Good*) have sold more copies of their books than I have. But their best-selling books were greatly influenced by my writings, as Dr. Burns has acknowledged.

Millions of readers and audio listeners have been directly helped by my works, as witnessed by thousands of direct verbal and written accolades I have received over the years. Further, since the 1980s I have been consistently voted one of the most influential psychologists by American and Canadian therapists.

Nevertheless, though I have published more than seventy-five professional and popular books and more than eight hundred articles, I have a long history of failure and censorship in writing—and some of it continues to the present day. First, my creative writing—my novels, plays, film scripts, poems, and songs—was never published at all. Up to my thirty-second year, in 1945, when the journal *Psychosomatic Medicine* published my first scientific article, "The Sexual Psychology of Human Hermaphrodites," I had written innumerable small pieces and twenty full-length book manuscripts, all of which were quickly rejected. I received several great criticisms—but nary an acceptance. In high school, starting at thirteen, I wrote my head off, but received only some awards in the New York World's Biggest News of the Week contest for students, but published nothing else till the age of thirty-two.

Undaunted, I wrote on and on. I was determined, among other things, to write the Great American Novel. Maybe I did—but it never even nearly got published. None of my five completed novels, nor my other fiction and nonfiction "masterpieces" were accepted until 1951, when my first book, *The Folklore of Sex*, was published by Charles Boni and Doubleday. By that time, I was already a man of thirty-eight.

Did I discourage myself about my hundreds of rejections? Not a bit. I wasn't in love with any publishers or journal editors; so I didn't think I *needed* their approval. As you can imagine, I felt very frustrated and disappointed about my constant rejections; but according to REBT, these are healthy negative emotions when Adversities occur in your life. I felt no unhealthy anxiety, depression, or anger. Maybe publishers and editors were wrong about rejecting my noble efforts—and I usually thought they were wrong. But, as we teach in REBT they had a right to be wrong, and that was bad but not awful. My rejections didn't make *me* a hopeless loser. My day—most probably!—would come.

I did, however, get some of my comic verses published in two columns in New York newspapers, but with no remuneration. The scores of verse that I sent to regular magazines like *The New Yorker* were all repeatedly rejected. Still, I was not desolate.

I finally agreed with the publishers that the *kind* of material I was writing would not sell too well, especially my books on political revolution and on organization. Besides, because of Stalin's tyrannical (and paranoid) rule in the Soviet Union, I gave up my devotion to collectivism, became much more democratic, and began to devote myself to sexual freedom. This seemed to represent *real* individualism and unique choice. You could, with the consent of particular partners, harmlessly enjoy yourself, as I began to do, with "free love." I also thought—wrongly!—that books on sex, love, and marriage with a liberal slant would be welcomed by publishers and would sell widely and wisely.

I therefore did enormous library research and consumed thousands—yes, thousands—of articles and books on sex, love, and marriage and began planning my masterpiece, *The Case for Promiscuity*. All the very bright and educated people in America, it seemed, were actively pursuing political revolution—stupidly, as Communists or fellow travelers—and practically everyone (except Bertrand Russell) was neglecting the most important sex and family revolution. Not I! I started mastering the vast amount of literature in the field, took home ten books from three public libraries every day, and swiftly skimmed through fifty to one hundred additional books on Saturday and Sunday at the famous Fifth Avenue and 42nd Street New York Public Library. I was well on my way. Then came the American Sexual Revolution! All this, while I divorced Karyl and *then* lived with her for a year. That was quite a revolution, too. While I shopped, cooked our food, and cleaned our apartment, she—allergic to such mundane tasks—agreed to type my sex, love, and marriage notes every day, and actually did so. I still have thousands of those notes and, through them, became perhaps the most outstanding authority on love, along with Pitorim Sorokin, in the world. Actually, I may have preceded him by a few years. Besides, he was a sexual prude, which belied his role as a specialist on sexuality.

I also included sex and marriage in my research and excelled in these respects, too. Unfortunately, the leading book publishers didn't agree. They liked my manuscripts, sometimes were enthusiastic, but didn't quite see that liberal—sometimes scorching—sex and love would sell in the 1930s. With publisher Lyle Stuart's help, I convinced them in the 1960s. But when I was first raring to go, they just weren't. Nothing published, nothing gained.

For fifteen more years, I got all my sex writings rejected. When my first published book, *The Folklore of Sex*, hit the presses in 1951, swiftly followed by a dozen other sex, love, and marriage books, I got some great reviews, little sales, and much censorship. Particularly, I received nonreviews and censorship of my publishers' ads in the "all the news that's fit to print" *New York Times*.

Was this censorship against me personally? I think so, but can't prove it, because the *Times* has always censored *liberal* sex, except for its kind treatment of homosexuality. But it has seriously neglected all my books, including those with little sex and much REBT. Was it stupid discrimination? Yes, in part. Perhaps personal animosity? Probably, because several times I protested their obvious prejudice against my writings.

Censorship wasn't limited to only the *Times*. As I indicate in my recent book, *Sex without Guilt for the Twenty-first Century*, my sex books have been ignored, railed against, and censored by the mass and professional media since 1951. The same is true for many of my professional writings, talks, radio and TV presentations, and workshops, which were not on sex, love, and marriage but were tarred by my sexual "reputation."

Let me give one illustration. I was scheduled to give an all-day workshop on REBT and disability at North Texas University. I was about to go to Denton, Texas, to give the workshop to several hundred professionals and students when some members of the Board of Directors of the university learned about my presentation two weeks before I was set to go and made the department of psychology cancel it. Why? Because of my terrible "sex reputation."

At first, in the 1950s, my sex and love books, mainly published by Lyle Stuart—who is an ardent advocate of free speech—didn't particularly sell until Grove Press, Dell Publications, and Bantam Books reprinted them in paperback form in the 1960s. Then *Sex without Guilt, The Art and Science of Love, The Sensuous Person*, and some of my other sex books began to make the best-seller lists. In the Americas and abroad millions of copies were sold to actual *readers*—probably more than Alfred Kinsey's books were actually *read*. My books were also widely quoted—with and without credit! This meant:

1. Good income for the Institute
2. Much less sex guilt for the public
3. Much better reputation for me by the public
4. Both good and bad reputation for the profession

5. Some publishers *asking* me to write sex books
6. Strong attacks against me by sex conservatives and prudes
7. Confusion of my sex views with my REBT views
8. Many clients with sex and love problems referred and self-referred to me

From all this, how did I take the criticism that was (legitimately and illegitimately) leveled against me for my liberal (and sometimes revolutionary) sex views? Very well, I think. For many reasons and in several ways:

1. I consciously and deliberately became a sex revolutionist. I knew at the start that I would get little but calumny, so I expected what I got and thought that it *confirmed* my honest belief that America (and other lands) could well use a sexual revolution.
2. I was, for many years, opposed to political and sexual censorship, and enjoyed fighting it when it was leveled against me.
3. I was developing REBT from 1953 onward, when I started to get much criticism, and I therefore accepted the harsh reality that my views on psychotherapy would be mistakenly and unfairly criticized—as they should *be* when they *were*. Too bad! Why must life be fair?
4. I saw that I was being lambasted by pretty crazy people. Consider the source!
5. The criticism was bringing me and my writings to notable attention—and some extra sales! Not so bad.
6. I realized that REBT and the Institute (which was established in 1959) were being "unfairly" tarred and feath-

ered because of my views on sexuality , but that was one price I had to pay for being honest. I felt it was worth it.

7. My sexual language—especially the use of "fuck" and "shit"—was creating opposition. But my daring to use "obscenities" in public was another part of my helping to liberalize people and help make them face sexual realities. Again, it was well worth it!

8. I believed that gay men and women were exceptionally persecuted in the 1950s, and I was more than willing to risk censure to help remove prejudice against them.

For these and other reasons, I continued my sexual crusade—and began to win more adherents to my cause, with the help of more respectable liberals, like Kinsey, Masters and Johnson, and Alex Comfort. Eventually, we became something of a majority by determinedly fighting the existing majority.

What happened with my liberal views on homosexuality in the 1940s and 1950s? Ironically, from both sides of the fence, I was lambasted. I began showing that much of what we call "sexual abnormality" and "sexual perversion" was odd but not by any means "wrong" or "disturbed" choices. Highly promiscuous, "deviated," and gay people often had "normal" tendencies to follow their sexual paths, and they often got into trouble (in our culture) for doing so. But if they chose to risk it, they were seldom punished and jailed, as long as they stuck to having sex-love relations with consenting adults.

I largely took this view from Havelock Ellis, Bertrand Russell, Magnus Hirschfeld, and other liberals of the late-nineteenth and early-twentieth centuries; and I held it in plainer language than most of them did. At first, I won few

friends and influenced few people with my honesty and direct-
ness. But I courageously continued.

My views on homosexuality particularly got me into
trouble. I said that gay people should be able to choose whatever kind of sex-love relations they preferred—barring, of
course, children and mentally deficient adults. So, together
with fighting antinudist restrictions, I saved a number of gays
from entrapment and sentencing for behaving homosexually.
I finally had to stop defending them in court because the pros-
ecuting attorneys began reading to the jury liberal passages
from my own books which "proved" that, although I was a
PhD with expertise in clinical and sexual psychology, I was
lewd and obscene and not in the least to be trusted.

Meanwhile, because of my liberal views on gayness, I
became an important part of the early gay liberation movement, an honorary member of the pioneering Mattachine
Society, and a close friend of Edward Sagain. He wrote a
famous book, *The Homosexual in America* (to which I wrote the
introduction), and he was the most prominent gay person in
the country.

Like myself, Ed was exceptionally liberal sexually but also
faced the fact that gay people were often emotionally disturbed, partly because of the ways in which they were persecuted but also because of their reckless actions in an antigay
society. He, like I, believed that they often largely chose their
sexual orientation, failed to acknowledge how risky it was in
their culture, and refused to practice it in a safe, private
manner. Because he publicly stated that many gays (like many
straight people) were disturbed, Ed was practically run out of
the gay liberation movement in the 1960s.

So was I. I pointed out, from clinical and research material, that gays, just like straights, were usually "normal" sexually, in that they chose sex acts—except penile-vaginal intercourse—that could easily be done with male or female partners (and sometimes with animals); however, they still rigidly eliminated many other sex partners, and therefore were prejudiced and quite self-restrictive, and consequently somewhat disturbed. When I said this, all hell broke loose, and most straight and gay people not only thought me sadly mistaken—which I well may have been—but also immoral and damnable. Pretty clever of me, wasn't it, to manage to be hated by most confirmed heterosexuals and homosexuals? Anyway, both exclusive straights and gays, who are the majority of humans, often did their best to denigrate me.

I naturally didn't like the prejudice against me—and still don't. But I took it the same way I take serious objections by many therapists to REBT. Sometimes they are right—for all therapies are highly imperfect, and often wrong or ineffective. But I think that REBT is considerably "right" and more effective than any of the other systems. So I accept the criticisms of other therapists and sometimes heed them and change some parts of REBT. But when they excoriate me, along with my views, I see them as foolishly overgeneralizing (see Korzybski again) and don't feel insulted or hurt. (Eleanor Roosevelt: "No one can insult you without your permission!")

My sex views have landed me in more trouble than any of my other teachings. They may be mistaken, even in some ways harmful. But no matter *what* people say, I, Albert Ellis, *am* not my *views*. I really believe that, and don't put my *self* down for often being damned for having them.

10.

DEALING WITH DAMNATION FOR MY ATHEISTIC VIEWS

It's about time I dealt with my atheism, which, along with my sexual views, has engendered more damnation of me than anything else. Strong religionists often are damners—as I would have expected. They often consign you to hell for disbelieving what they devoutly believe.

However, not all devout religionists are dangerous. I have also been blessed many times by "liberal" Christians who fully hold the doctrines of accepting the sinner (Albert Ellis) but not his sins (atheism) and who lovingly bless me in spite of my damnable views.

I became a firm atheist at the age of twelve, while I was studying Hebrew and preparing for my bar mitzvah. Before that, I had been only moderately religious—when, as I have noted, I was afflicted with a "terrible" headache.

By the time I was twelve, I largely followed Bertrand Russell by thinking myself out of all religions and supernatural beliefs and becoming what I called a "probabilistic atheist." My definition of this included the following ideas:

1. God and the supernatural obviously—as Kant said in *The Critique of Pure Reason*—cannot be proven or disproven. To absolutely "prove" their existence is obviously dogmatism, which I strongly oppose, as a real contradiction!

2. Although we can have no *certainty* that God does or does not exist, we have an exceptionally high degree of probability that He or She doesn't. This is exactly the same degree we have in thinking that there *most probably* is no Santa Claus, no fairies, no angels, and no devil. There could be—but it is most improbable.

3. I prefer, therefore, to be an atheist, not an agnostic. Agnostics hold that they do not *know* if God exists and prefer to remain ignorant. No one *really* knows, so they accept uncertainty. I go one step further. I can't *prove* that Santa Claus and angels don't exist, but I firmly believe they don't. I recognize that there is such a low degree of probability—something like .000000001 percent—that Santa Claus exists but I assume, for all practical purposes, that he doesn't. Then I have *no* trouble.

4. Of course, as a probabilist, I logically have to face the "fact" that powerful supernatural Gods and other entities *could* exist and (being unpredictable) *could* punish me for *dis*believing in them. Most improbable. But they *could* roast me (very unlikely) in hell.

What then? Then, I tell myself, if so I'll face it and roast in hell for eternity. That's pretty bad—but not *awful*. I tell my clients in our early sessions this story. "Here's a true story. We've had an excellent REBT practitioner for twenty years with a PhD in clinical psychology, who is also a priest of the Mormon Church. He teaches psychology at a leading Mormon university. He tells his students that the Mormon Scriptures—not the Christian Bible—clearly say that if they choose to be gay, they roast in hell for eternity. I don't know what happens to them if they are non-Mormons; but if they are Mormons and gay, they definitely roast in hell for eternity. 'But,' he then adds, following REBT and its philosophy, 'that's not *awful*. It's only *highly inconvenient!*'"

So, as I also sometimes tell my clients, "If a punishing God ignores REBT principles and damns me to hell for eternity, I expect to rule down there and make sure that I and everyone else has a fucking good time!"

As I do in this life, I go by the laws of probability and fully convince myself that nothing supernatural exists. But if in one out of a hundred trillion chances it does, I'll live with it. After figuring this out at the age of twelve, I began to tell everyone—even my beautiful Hebrew teacher at my temple, with whom I was madly in love—that I was definitely an atheist instead of an agnostic. She and many others were rather horrified; and I still often get letters from all over the world damning me for my "stupid" stand. As ever, too bad. I happily go my atheistic way.

I have changed in one important respect and made a startling confession at the 1997 Annual Convention of the American Psychological Association in Chicago. Previously, in 1969, I had written the famous—and infamous—article, "The Case

Against Religiosity" for Lyle Stuart's (also infamous) newspaper the *Independent*. I really hauled it over the coals and concluded:

> To summarize: Conventional religion is, on many counts, directly opposed to the main goals of emotional health— since it basically consists of masochism, other-directedness, intolerance, refusal to accept ambiguity and uncertainty, unscientific thinking, needless inhibition, and self- abasement. Are all religious individuals, then, seriously dis- turbed? No, because many who think of themselves as reli- gious—such as the Reformed Jews, the Liberal Protestants, and the Buddhists—*selectively* accept only the reasonably sane ethical principles and philosophic views of their reli- gion and do not dogmatically believe in almost any of its aspects. They are still somewhat childishly dependent on their assumed Gods; but not too seriously so. On the other hand, true believers in just about *any* kind of orthodoxy— whether it be religious, political, social, or even artistic orthodoxy—tend to be distinctly disturbed, since they are obviously rigid, fanatic, and dependent individuals. Reli- gion, as noted in the beginning of this paper, is a vague term today; but religiosity, or the quality of being extremely or excessively religious, is less open to interpretation. True believerism (to use Eric Hoffer's term) or religiosity (which I consider to be synonymous with it) is the central core of conventional religion. And religiosity, by my estimation, is another name for narrow-mindedness, emotional distur- bance, or neurosis. Or, in some extreme cases, psychosis!

In 1983, I gave some more thought to the place of religion in mental health. I concluded that it was not religion and a belief in the supernatural that was the real culprit. Instead, it is what I called *religiosity*: "a devout or rigid belief in some kind of secular religion (such as Libertarianism, Marxism, or Freudianism)—that is, a dogmatic, absolutistic conviction that some political, economic, social, or philosophical view is sacrosanct, provides ultimate answers to virtually all important questions, and is to be piously subscribed to and followed by everyone who wishes to lead a good life." My revised article, "The Case Against Religiosity," was published in 1983 by the Albert Ellis Institute and by American Atheists.

I thought that my case against religiosity—not merely against religion—would be my final word on this subject. Not at all! I gave it more deep thought and was informed about the work of Steven Nielsen and W. Brad Johnson, two Christian psychologists (and REBTers) who presented evidence that devout faith in Christianity and other leading religions could be *helpfully* held by many people.

True. Even if it can be factually shown that both religious and secular dogma and devoutness tend to wreak great harm on us humans, it can also be shown beyond a reasonable doubt that such rigid beliefs can *sometimes* help people mentally and emotionally. Although a paradoxical concept, it is still (sometimes) true.

Oddly enough, this realization is actually an intrinsic part of REBT theory. As Epictetus (a pagan philosopher) wisely observed two thousand years ago, it is not unfortunate and undesirable events that disturb people, but their *views* about such events. Gautama Buddha and other philosophers were similar constructivists. So, with some reservations, am I.

REBT holds, in other words, that it is *commonly* but not

always true that irrational, unrealistic, and illogical beliefs help create dysfunctional and undesirable feelings and behaviors. Sometimes the reverse occurs. Thus, if you are prone to "irrational" beliefs (as just about all humans are) you may be distinctly happy as a result of them—and may even help yourself ward off the ravages of innate and socially learned depression. Suppose, for example, you believe in the devil and are certain that the devil favors you and will make your life good. Is it irrational? From logical and scientific standpoints, most probably yes. But completely harmful to you? Most probably no.

Moral: We'd better not dogmatically, inflexibly, and at all times hold that irrational beliefs are harmful to our goals of being happy and effective. Usually or often? Yes. Invariably? No.

My views on the harm of inflexible, dogmatic, and rigid secular and nonreligiosity have now changed somewhat, though not completely. I still think that this kind of extreme believing often "causes" immense physical and mental harm. Especially if *harm* itself can be accurately agreed upon by humans—which is extremely difficult! Dogmatic views of "harm" and "benefit" also have their dangers.

I wrote a book with Steven Nielsen and Brad Johnson, *Counseling and Psychology with Religious Persons*, that shows how Christian and other profound religious views can be used by REBT practitioners. But I have also rewritten my 1968 book on Ayn Rand and have titled it *Ayn Rand: Her Fascistic and Fanatically Religious Philosophy*. Read both these books and see what my negative attitude is now toward fanaticism in religion—and in almost anything.

Let's return, again, to people's attitudes toward me. Perhaps my more *tolerant* views on devout religiosity have led some of my detractors to call off their dogs. Prejudice against my views is quite okay. But prejudice against and damnation of *me* for holding them is quite another dish. I still don't like it, but, with REBT, bear up nicely with it. Many of my readers and listeners still damn my views *and* me. I really don't damn them back and sometimes benefit from their violent denunciations. Let us hope I shall continue to do so.

11.

COPING WITH MY POOR EYESIGHT

One problem that plagued me for about sixty years of my life was optical disability. For my first nineteen years, I saw reasonably well and then, when I got my first pair of glasses, even better. Not long after, my eyes kept getting tired after an hour or so of reading. No ophthalmologist could tell why or what to do about it.

One, at Columbia University's clinic, finally said—after hearing about the failures of other leading ophthalmologists to properly diagnose and treat me—that my disability resulted from my frailness, general weakness, and lack of fresh air and exercise. He may have been partly right, but his prescription—more fresh air and exercise—never worked. My eyes still got easily tired and it often felt like there was sand in them—similar problems to those that my brother, Paul, experienced twenty years later.

One thing was highly suspicious—my renal glycosuria. I was afflicted with type 1 insulin-dependent diabetes at the age of forty, though it wasn't fully diagnosed until five years later. When I started having boils, at age forty, I read *Merck's Manual* —a great self-help book—cut down on eating fats and carbohydrates, and apparently kept my diabetes under control until I was forty-five and routine checkups at Columbia-Presbyterian Medical Center found the culprit.

At nineteen, however, medical checkups found that I had renal glycosuria—too much sugar in my urine but *not* in my blood. So for the next twenty years, I was careful about my sugar intake. Regardless, there was no letup of my easily tired eyes. So I used several practical adjustments. (1) I closed my eyes often, especially at lectures and when listening (very often) to music. (2) I told friends and girlfriends about my disability and frequently closed my eyes when conversing with them. (3) At work, I did several different kinds of tasks, which relieved my eyestrain a bit. I also talked a good deal on the phone, with my eyes tightly closed. (4) When I started to practice psychotherapy at the age of forty-three, I told my clients about my ocular disability and also told them that I could concentrate better on their problems with my eyes closed—which was true. (5) I became *un*addicted to TV and films, and largely "viewed" them by listening much of the time with my eyes closed.

There was always a hassle and adjustments! But I nicely got by. In *that* respect, I taught myself high frustration tolerance (HFT) and what I later called unconditional life-acceptance (ULA). I did this with no whining whatsoever.

As with my frequent headaches, there was no diagnosis or proper medical treatment. Years later, as I noted about my headaches, keeping my blood sugar consistently low—by testing it ten times a day—relieved both my headaches and, partly, my tired eyes. I am not sure, but I think that cured me.

Meanwhile, I coped and coped with my disability. First, I had invented shame-attacking exercises in my early twenties—as I show elsewhere in this book. While almost everyone I knew thought it most peculiar when I conversed with my eyes closed, I used my shame-attacking exercises and outlook to agree with them, but not feel at all ashamed or humiliated by shutting my eyes. As far as I could see, they all took my peculiarity well and only a few made themselves insulted by my lack of looking at them in the eyes. Good riddance!

Second, as noted above, I deplored my disability but resiliently accepted it. In fact, even when it largely got better—ironically, as I became older—I often indulged in closing my eyes when I didn't have to. I took advantage of my more relaxed state, with my eyes closed, and the greater concentration powers it gave me.

Of all my physical handicaps, then, my sixty-year spell of tired eyes theoretically gave me more trouble than most of my other failings. But because of my rational attitudes toward it, which I formed prior to creating REBT, I coped with it and turned it to an advantage with hard thinking and disciplined practice.

My eye problems are another example of HFT solution. My first pair of rimless glasses looked fine, but the nosepiece, with two pearl buttons, kept cutting into the sensitive skin of my nose, causing fairly steady pain and leading me to put some lubrication on the bridge of my nose every night before I went to sleep. Still, steady irritation persisted. I kept trying to talk my optician and my friends into my getting a less attractive frame for my glasses, but they were adamant, and I stupidly bought their esthetic views. After a couple of years, I stopped that crap, insisted on fully framed glasses that are not *so* esthetic, and have solved the problem completely. So some of my girlfriends keep objecting. Unfuck them!

12.

COPING WITH SEX SHAME AND OTHER SHAME

I probably should have worked on my sex shame when I was twelve and began to get huge erections every day, which might well show through my pants and brand me as some kind of a "pervert." I especially didn't want one of the girls I was in love with to see my erections and kept crossing my legs tightly to keep them from being viewed. I had them in class, during sports, and while socializing with my male friends. But, fortunately, I learned from some of the boys' *unembarrassed* and joking remarks that I was hardly alone and not *too* "perverted." My hormones were in great shape and I "knew" that no one had as many—much *too* many—erections as I. Damn! I did my best to hide them and to not put myself down *too* much for my "perversions."

I also was addicted, from fifteen years onward, to a real, socially disapproved problem—frotteurism. I discovered it accidentally, when on a crowded subway train on the way home from school, a not-too-attractive teenage girl kept pushing her ass against my midsection until—what do you know!—I flowingly came. How shameful! Though no one seemed to see my wet pants—or seemed to care if they did see, I knew I was "immoral" because I thereafter sought out crowded trains, standing room in the back of movie theaters, crowded elevators, and other places where I could rub my midsection against women's backsides and hips and soon get delicious orgasms. Since at that time I was too shy to date girls, this was an easy, comfortable outlet; and I even used condoms to prevent myself from wetting my dratted pants.

Gratification was easy, and, as I soon found, not very risky and immoral. I almost always found girls and women who liked my pressing against their asses and loins—indeed, who frequently *sought* to help me do it, even in not-so-crowded trains and other places. My friend Manny, who with my brother was the only one I told about my subway exploits, fully confirmed my observations. Even though he was somewhat fat and unprepossessing, he had countless frotteur adventures—as did I. Some women, including middle-aged women, sought him out!

I was really very polite, and never bothered a girl or woman who gave any indication that she didn't want to be bothered. One negative glance or push away from me and I immediately withdrew—often to try another woman! I knew, however, that I was "taking advantage" of a few women—and that that was wrong and immoral. That didn't stop me from trying. Over the years, until I had "regular" sex with consenting partners, I had hundreds of frotteur-incited sex adventures. So I was hardly abstinent!

One woman, for instance, about thirty-five years of age and wearing a wedding ring, planned to take the same subway train I usually took to work every morning, deliberately stayed on the empty platform at the end of the train until it filled up with people, and then she—and I—maneuvered to get close together and dry-fucked until we both gloriously came. What fun!

One day, by accident, I met her on the way home and sat next to her in an uncrowded car—whereupon she practically sat in my lap. As usual, we said nothing to each other. I followed her to her apartment house, went up in the elevator to her floor, and was about to follow her into the apartment when she smilingly said, "No you can't go in. I have a husband and two young children." So I peacefully left—to resume our regular morning sex until, finally, she quit her job and I saw her no more.

Subway sex was the cheapest and easiest sex I ever had, and I continued it into my twenties, when I started to have "regular" sex with Karyl and several other women. But in some ways, it was great: no fuss, no obligations, no time wasted, no having to put up with the inane conversation of most women, no pregnancy, no disease, no boredom. Though it was not as good as being in bed with a naked woman (but not as hassled, either). It didn't interfere at all with my working and creative life. I still endlessly wrote—for an audience of one, myself.

I knew that frotteurism was wrong—that it is sometimes nonconsenting. I once heard a woman shout for ten minutes against another frotteur. But I completely rid myself of my shame at doing it. If done tactfully and politely, it was harmless, seldom an intrusion—and had all the advantages I listed in the previous paragraph. I was grateful to my anonymous partners—and was happy that I obviously pleased so many of them. *Bien!*—as we used to say in my French classes.

Working against my sex shame also led to my invention of my now-famous shame-attacking exercises at the age of twenty-three. First, I overcame my anxiety about selling, when I was in business with my brother, Paul, selling and matching pants. I got over the shame of approaching young women in the Bronx Botanical Gardens at the age of nineteen. This was greatly motivated by my strong refusal to risk trying to date them and horror of being rejected. But I still abhorred salesmanship because, according to my mother, my father, Henry, was so aggressive at it that he could, and practically did, sell anybody the Brooklyn Bridge. So when I had to make cold approaches to scores of store owners in our pants selling and matching business, I at first avoided doing so. I didn't want to intrude, to flimflam them, to get rejection after rejection. So I initially let Paul do the selling while I delivered the pants. Then Paul bought a secondhand tin lizzie and delivered pants better than I, and I agreed to do the approaching and selling.

At first I was very uncomfortable and apologetic for barging in on the customers. But having forced myself to do considerable in vivo desensitization in picking up women in the Bronx Botanical Gardens, I forced myself to do it again with store owners—and soon lost my shame and, being a fluent talker, made myself into an excellent salesman. In fact, I made friends with many of the storekeepers—especially those who were left-wingers, who noticed my carrying around the latest copy of

The New Masses and had long talks with me in those (very political) days.

Once again, I became shameless. One thing, however, bothered me. I made many friends at Poe Park, a famous place two blocks from my home on Jerome Avenue, and saw them most nights of the week—particularly when I was trying to help create, first, the American political revolution and, second, the Great American Sexual Revolution. When I was with my friends, from about eight o'clock to midnight, we left the park for a cafeteria two blocks away to finish up the day. Almost all my friends were working and therefore had enough money for coffee and food at the cafeteria. But I was either not working or had little money from my business with Paul, so I often couldn't even afford a ten-cent piece of cheesecake.

I was thoroughly ashamed *not* to afford it. We took a ticket when we entered the cafeteria and had to pay for our food on the way out. Either the regular cashier was there or the owner of the place—both of whom I knew very well. So I was thoroughly ashamed to face them and present my blank ticket, which showed that I had not taken any food. I (foolishly) thought it "disgraceful" to use their cafeteria for an hour and not pay anything. After all, what did they run the cafeteria for—nothing?

Every time I went, I *made* myself get some food—usually only ten cents' worth—and pay on the way out. I did this time after time, with perhaps my last ten cents. Could I let them—and my friends—know I was a cheapskate? Never!

I knew, of course, that my behavior was "crazy." I knew I had by no means overcome my "idiotic" feelings of shame. Come what may, I was determined to continue going to the cafeteria, especially as my idiocy dragged on and on.

To fix things, I invented, in my early twenties, my shame-attacking exercise. I knew—mainly from reading psychology—that I cared *too much* about what people thought of me—and therefore made myself ashamed of "intruding on" or "displeasing" them.

For example, whenever I had to urinate, I always looked for a Horn and Hardart cafeteria to do so. They had open bathrooms which you could use without buying any food, or, if you wanted food, could get nickels to put in their food slots and never be seen by any cashier while using the bathroom.

Well, I decided to risk it and change all that. I would deliberately, consciously *let myself* be observed by "dangerous" observers, and would make myself not give a damn about their potential interference and criticism. To hell with it—sticks and stones might break my bones, but from now on people's names would never—never!—hurt me.

For the next few months, I went blithely around New York doing "shameful," "risky" things. I'd go to a cafeteria, take a ticket, take a glass of water or go to the bathroom, and give the cashier my empty ticket. Did she glare, make a negative remark, or otherwise object to my "free ride"? She sometimes did. Let her object!

Actually, I knew the law, which said that a "public carrier" like a restaurant had to serve you water without any charge—unless it had (like Stewart's cafeteria in Greenwich Village) a sign outside stating that it had a minimum cover charge. So I pointed this out to a few bellicose cashiers and easily won the day.

I did the same thing in office buildings. I deliberately asked the elevator starters where the nearest men's room was. "Fourth floor," they'd reply. I went to that floor, used the men's room, came down again, thanked the elevator starter, and left. I felt no shame.

Within a few weeks of practicing scores of shame-attacking exercises, I had real "chutzpah" and felt unembarrassed about doing practically anything (nothing illegal, I made sure). I didn't want *real* jeopardy, but I did all kinds of things that led to all kinds of looks. I felt delighted that I was fast overcoming *my* foolish fears.

Years later, when I did psychotherapy with scores—nay, hundreds—of clients who had social anxiety, I urged them to do many harmless things they were horribly afraid of doing; and in the 1960s I invented my shame-attacking exercise and publicized it widely. I have successfully used this with thousands of clients and readers. Often, they feel that it is the most useful tool in the REBT armamentarium. Here is how I describe it in one of my latest books, *Overcoming Resistance: A Rational Emotive Behavior Integrative Approach.*

USING SHAME-ATTACKING EXERCISES

The shame-attacking exercises that I developed in the 1960s are one of the best known and most useful of the emotive-evocative and behavioral REBT methods for helping people surrender their strong self-downing tendencies. In so calling them, I realized that what we normally call *shaming* is the essence of a great deal of human disturbance. It is not by any means the only human tendency that leads people to upset themselves and also to further upset themselves about their upsetness. As I have already pointed out, low frustration tolerance also contributes mightily to their becoming and remaining upset. But self-denigrating or blaming oneself for one's failings, particularly when one exhibits them in the presence of other judging individuals, is hard to beat as a method for sabotaging oneself.

When people feel what is usually called shame, embarrassment, or humiliation, especially when they have acted foolishly or incompetently in the presence of others, they usually acknowledge two things. First, they see that they did "badly" or "wrongly" and that others observed this and agree that they acted "badly." Second, they do not merely acknowledge their errors and ineptness, but they also judge *themselves*, and usually damn their *personhood* for having done it. They of course can experience self-shaming and self-embarrassing when they are not in social situations, because they can notice their own incompetent behaviors and can excoriate themselves for them. But even when they are being severely criticized by others and even when these others are trying to make them feel ashamed, they themselves are contributing mightily to the process. As Eleanor Roosevelt said, "No one can insult you without your permission."

Recognizing that self-shaming is ubiquitous among humans and that it has serious emotional consequences—because one can easily continue denigrating oneself long after the so-called shameful act has ended—I developed several ways of helping my clients overcome it. Most notable of these are, shame-attacking exercises, which I have assigned to hundreds of clients and encouraged thousands more in my talks and writings to use to effectively tackle their self-shaming. Those who have pushed themselves to regularly do them report having benefited considerably and learned to greatly reduce their social anxiety.

Shame-attacking is also one of the best ways to teach clients one of the basic theories of REBT. For when they tell me, usually in the first few sessions, that they did something "stupid" and that that "made" them feel ashamed, or that another person "made" them feel humiliated, I quickly stop them and say, "That's really impossible. No one can make you feel almost anything—except with a baseball bat. You control your inner states of feeling." And frequently I cite Eleanor Roosevelt's maxim.

I do, of course, go on to explain that I am not in the least denying their *feelings* of humiliation. I am simply showing them that when they acted "idiotically," and other people mocked them for doing so, they had a *choice* of feeling the *healthy* feelings of sorrow, regret, and annoyance or the *unhealthy* feelings of shame, embarrassment, and humiliation. In making the latter choice, they told themselves, once they noticed (or imagined) their "wrong" behavior and others' disapproval, (1) "I am behaving wrongly, stupidly, or badly and being judged by others for doing so," and (2), "that makes me a shameful, idiotic, and inadequate person!"

Many clients are able to see this fairly quickly and begin to get it into their heads and hearts. At least, they see it lightly—that is, *acknowledge* that they are doing so. But it usually takes them a while to start to really undo their feelings of shame by regularly zeroing in on and disputing their self-denigrating musts.

When I show my clients this REBT theory of self-shaming, they usually see it and work a bit on it. But many of them, particularly the most resisting ones, strongly condemn themselves for their social disabilities and have an extremely difficult time refraining from doing so. This is because they have been biologically predisposed, socially taught, and have practiced self-blaming and its correlative self-shaming for a good many years, and often have had trouble giving it up. I therefore explain to them the rationale of the shame-attacking exercise and try to induce them to do at least one of them as a homework assignment. I say something like the following:

"Shaming is the essence of a great deal of human disturbing. It largely consists of first doing some foolish or incompetent behavior and noticing that you do it; second, realizing that others may be condemning you for it; and third, agreeing with others' (real or imagined) condemnation. 'Because I acted foolishly, I am a totally stupid, silly, incompetent person.' In other words, you may be rightly downing your behavior, but you are wrongly downing your total self, your being, your essence for doing that behaving. I want you to be able to see this very clearly and one of the ways to see it is to do a shame-attacking exercise.

"If you do the following exercise, you will clearly see your own tendency to defame yourself and will, I hope, be encouraged to stop rating yourself globally. So think of something that you would consider very shameful and humiliating. Some of the most frequently used shame attacks are getting on the bus and yelling out the stops at the top of your lungs (and staying on the bus and trying to not feel ashamed). Or you can go to a department store and loudly shout out the time: 'Ten thirty-three and all's well!' Or you can go to a hotel lobby or some popular meeting place, stop a stranger, and say, 'I just got out of the loony bin. What month is it?' Or you can walk a banana on a red leash and feed it with another banana.

"So try one of these actions, or try one that you yourself would feel particularly ashamed of if you did it. Don't do it as a joke and for amusement, but really pick something that you would feel quite embarrassed to do and do it in public where other people can see you and stare or laugh at you. This may not change your whole life, but I can almost guarantee that if you keep doing these exercises several times, you will begin to see that you are the shamer of yourself and that nobody else can make you feel humiliated. You have the choice of feeling sorry and regretful if people look askance at you or feeling anxious and depressed. You are probably habituated to feeling shame and anxiety instead of regret and concern; I would like to see you break out of this pattern. How do you feel about doing this exercise?"

My clients are often quite amused at the idea of doing a shame-attacking exercise, yet also very anxious. They likely see that it may well do them a lot of good and help them counterattack their self-downing. But that hardly makes them do it. A few of them actually go out and do one or more shame-attacking exercises immediately. But they are usually the ones who somehow throw some humor into it and do it partly as a lark. If I keep after them, most are able to do a number of shame-attacking exercises and almost always benefit somewhat doing it; many wind up making remarkable progress in reducing shame and self-consciousness.

I usually give shame-attacking exercise to my four therapy groups at least once a year. Each member picks her or his own particular exercise to do, commits to doing it within the next week, and reports back to the group on it. Many of the members—especially those who have been in REBT for a while and already done some—fairly readily agree. Other members are very recalcitrant and may outrightly refuse, but older group members encourage them to try one exercise during the week and report back on it.

Some time ago, I had in group a very shy twenty-five-year-old male who avoided all social engagements and particularly ones where he might meet a woman to whom he was attracted. As a result, his social life was practically nil. When I gave this group the shame-attack homework, he refused, especially to agreeing to do something that would be socially disapproved. But the group and I finally convinced him to do one of our favorites.

To get the agony over with, he went out onto Sixty-fifth Street, right outside our Institute, and approached a very well dressed man from an expensive apartment house across the street. "I just got out of the mental hospital," he said to the man. "What month is it?" The man looked at him in shock and obviously thinking that he was completely crazy, scooted quickly away from him. But when he saw that he was able to do the exercise, and that it was easier than he had thought, he felt exhilarated. He wound up doing about twenty more shame-attacks with different people, particularly ones who looked snooty or affluent, and had the best week, socially, of his entire life. He was so successful in sabotaging his self-sabotaging limitations that within the next few weeks he began to regularly make social overtures to attractive women.

Everything, of course, does not turn out that well. I had another client who stopped somebody in the subway and said, "I just got out of the loony bin. What month is it?" And the individual he stopped angered himself so much that he actually slightly pushed my client. I warn clients, however, not to impose too much on others, and certainly not to frighten or harm them in any way, such as poking them in the back. I also warn them not to do anything (such as taking off their clothes in the street) that will get them in trouble with the police or other authorities. Although I have heard from thousands of people doing shame-attacking exercises, I have yet to hear about anyone who has gotten into any serious trouble.

Clients often have strong biological as well as social learning foundations. Consequently, you show them with REBT and CBT methods that they are partly responsible for their own disturbances: that feeling ashamed is a natural human tendency and that they can learn to change it by insight and hard work.

In other words, you can teach your clients that while they construct a good deal of their disturbed behaviors, they can also see how destructive this behavior is and implement changes. The ability to change one's dysfunctional thoughts, feelings, and behaviors, even when one has helped create them for many years, is one of the essences of being human. As a therapist, even though you are showing your clients that they have a good deal of responsibility for choosing—or not choosing—to be distinctly bollixed up about Adversities, you are helping instill in them an optimistic, self-accepting, and creative outlook.

13.

THE CENSORSHIP OF
MY FIRST PhD THESIS

Perhaps the worst kind of sex-related censorship I ever experienced was in 1946, when I was thirty-three years old and writing my PhD thesis at Columbia University. Already being something of an authority on love—personally and professionally—I picked as my thesis topic, "A Study of the Love Relationships of Women." My thesis adviser, Percival Symonds, and the committee accepted the topic.

I enjoyed working on the study I was doing. It involved interviewing young women, whom I easily contacted—since practically all the women in the Bronx and Manhattan were inhibited about discussing the details of their sex lives but enjoyed talking about their love emotions and relationships. I talked to them and gave them a questionnaire I had devised, got all my material in order, was approved by thesis seminars, and was about to write my final thesis when the ax fell.

Two leading professors—a man and a woman—found out about my study, and protested that the sensation-loving newspapers of New York—the *Mirror* and the *Journal-American* (both, at times, Hearst papers) would discover it and write "Columbia Student Writes Thesis on Love!" Who knows what they would say? Teachers College, my clinical psychology school, and Columbia University would be tarred as "liberal" or even "radical"—and they wouldn't like that.

A furor was raised and a special seminar was arranged, including all the leading Teachers College and Columbia professors of psychology and counseling, plus the provost of Columbia, who I didn't even know existed up to that time. Thirteen of them would attend, I would describe my findings to date, and they would decide if I could proceed with my thesis.

The special seminar met at the end of 1946 and decided eleven to thirteen in my favor. I was a scholar, and my proposed thesis was on a valid topic that was being scientifically conducted. I agreed with the seminar committee. But, but, but. My new adviser, the famous Goodwin Watson, substituting for the out-of-town Percival Symonds, regretfully informed me that the two dissenting professors had told him that if I had the audacity to continue my "vile" study, they would oppose me and it to the bitterest end. Even if I did an impersonal study on love—like a comparison of love emotions in the novels of the nineteenth and twentieth centuries—they would make sure that they knocked it down at my final hearing on my thesis. With their "help," I would never get a degree from Columbia, no matter how good everyone else found my thesis.

Goodwin strongly advised me to get an entirely different—and totally uncontroversalist—topic for my thesis. I saw immediately that he was right.

Although Goodwin did not inform me who the two dissidents were, I easily figured out their identities. One was a leading professor of psychology and an unattractive "old maid" who was reputed to have had no sex or love affairs in her sixty-five years, and who in her teaching and writings was notoriously prudish. I suspected her before I started work on my thesis and went to ask her permission to work on it. After reading my proposal, she said, "Mr. Ellis, I know you as a student and know what fine work you do." She had given me two A's in her counseling courses and commended my term papers highly. "I have carefully read your proposal for your thesis, and find that you have done it very well and that it is a legitimate scientific study." She paused for a moment, looked at me out of her steely blue eyes, and said, "But do you really think that anyone at all is seriously interested in love?"

I could hardly believe what she was saying—but I finally managed to believe it of *her*. Dry-mouthed, I said, "Yes, maybe you're right. I'll think about it."

"Do," she finished. Knowing all the other professors I spoke to before this—including Carney Landis, a backer of Alfred Kinsey and an authority himself on sex—I decided to pursue my study of love—but not as a Columbia thesis.

But not now, with Goodwin's advice that if I did *anything* on love, the two dissidents would finally get me by finding *some* reasons why my thesis was "unsuitable." They *would*. I immediately decided to give up my thesis, publish my findings in psychological and sociological journals, and pick another *very safe* topic.

I was interested in paper-and-pencil personality tests, which I wrote a scathing review of in the very respectable *Psychological Bulletin*, "The Validity of Personality Questionnaires" in 1946. But I thought that projective techniques of testing people's personality were basically Freudian and consequently *more* unreliable than nonprojective methods. So I decided to test my hypothesis and began working on "A Comparison of the Use of Direct Phrasing in Personality Questionnaires," that was published in *Psychological Monographs* in 1947.

That *almost* ended my thesis troubles. Unfortunately, however, I had no help with the new statistical technique, analysis of variance, because my fine adviser, Helen Walker, was out of the country on sabbatical leave. So I taught it to myself, being good at statistics, conquered it, but made a mistake adding one column of figures vertically instead of horizontally.

It is too much for me to go into the details here, but the clinical psychology department of Teachers College, Columbia University, where I was officially registered, had a feud with the academic psychology department of Columbia, across 120th Street, where I also took many courses. Both departments childishly tried to sabotage the other's students at the final PhD thesis orals, where members of both were always present. I therefore was at that time a victim of academic Columbia. My thesis was about to be approved by the orals committee when Joseph Zubin, a brilliant psychologist—and a friend of mine—reported that he had gone through it with a calculator, found my error, and saw that one of my main conclusions (in favor of direct instead of indirect wording of personality questionnaires) was partly wrong.

Academic Columbia was definitely winning over clinical

Teachers College, and I was presumably screwed. I saw right away that Zubin was right and was about to apologize and correct my error, when the world-famous Irving Lorge jumped in and disputed Zubin. Lorge, who had deliberately given me a hard time in my pre-orals seminars, in order to prepare me for "those bastards" at Columbia psychology, now emphatically declared that I was right and that Zubin was wrong: that no one yet knew enough about the techniques of analysis of variance to say whether I was wrong, and that I was an outstanding scholar who deserved my degree. Being a little more palliative, he said he would personally go over the thesis with me and, if necessary, would make some corrections to it.

This created an impasse, especially since Robert Thorndike (son of Edward Thorndike, one of the geniuses in psychology), who was also a Teachers College and not a Columbia mainspring, said that he, too, had used a computer to go through my thesis (which probably was a lie) and that Zubin was unquestionably right and I and Lorge were *very* wrong.

I, however, had been counseling Lorge about his personal and marital problems when we were presumably conferring about my thesis; and he was solving his problems and becoming pretty happy instead of (usually) irascible. Because of my helpful counseling, or because of his insistent backing of Teachers College over Columbia, Irving went into a resplendent, uninterruptible accolade of me and my (poor) thesis—and won. It was quickly decided, as he insisted, that I forthright be awarded my PhD and that I confer with him about possibly reviewing part of it. So be it. I was off the hook.

How did I emotionally take all of this? Very well. I decided, while still talking to Goodwin Watson, that my thesis on love was outstanding but, for practical reasons, was dead as a cinder—for the nonce. I buried it and quickly came up with my new topic on the differences between projective and non-projective personality tests. I induced Gertrude, with whom I was still madly in love, to give my tests to her junior high school students. I learned analysis of variance, which I knew my orals board members did not know because of its newness. I hired a computer, a Mathemeton, and worked mainly at my office at Distinctive Creations during the day, whacking away at its noisy mechanism. I did all this—and more—from January to March 1947; passed my orals in April (as I have noted); and became a PhD (with knowledge that is officially Piled Higher and Deeper).

In the meantime, I experienced only feelings of disappointment and annoyance but had practically no anxiety, depression, anger, or low frustration tolerance (mainly because I strongly focused on the work to be done and the practical *advantages* of doing it, getting my PhD quickly, and then becoming a licensed psychologist). Were these pains in the ass to be hurdled? Definitely. Did I whine about others' bigotries and my own foolish errors? Definitely not. In fact, *decidedly* not because I deliberately *decided* to unupset myself.

Here I got closer to applying the pre-REBT philosophy that I had been working toward much of my life. First, I kept all my main goals, even when they were being most thwarted and blocked. I was determined from 1942 (when I was twenty-nine) onward to be a psychologist and psychotherapist and determined (meaning cognitively and emotionally) to have my emotional desires fulfilled. I never lost sight of or gave up on that.

Second, I kept actively (behaviorally) working toward that goal (PYA, or push your ass, as we say in REBT). I really kept pushing—with my professors, at my research, and at my thesis writing, at *modifying* my goals and purposes when necessary. I also worked at relating to Percival Symonds, Goodwin Watson, Irving Lorge, Gertrude, and others who might aid or block my goals.

Third, though I didn't clearly and consciously realize it at the time, I cognitively-emotionally sensed, figured out, and stuck to an early version of unconditional self-acceptance (USA) when I made stupid mistakes—as when I first picked the wrong thesis topic and later made some distinct errors when researching and writing the right one. I also partly thought out (cognitively-emotionally again) unconditional other-acceptance (UOA), never hated my *opponents* but just hated their *behaviors*.

Did I at that time use my latter-day philosophy of high frustration tolerance (HFT) and unconditional life-acceptance (ULA)? Again, pretty much so. I didn't damn the PhD-getting system, Teachers College's and Columbia University's setup, and the often unfair and unjust world. Once again, I greatly disliked them but—different from my former political revolutionary position—didn't decide to blow them up. This was impractical—and hardly worth my time. Besides, if I carefully watched and took advantage of it, the system under which I lived could *aid* my goals if I wisely used it.

14.

COPING WITH MY IRRITABILITY AND ANGER

I think I have vast reserves of irritability—just like my father, Henry. He was something of a bigoted conservative businessman who frequently hated (1) liberals and Democrats, (2) *Schvartzers* (African Americans), (3) restrictions on competition, (4) stupid people, (5) some of his close relatives, (6) myriads of awful conditions. Don't get me wrong, however; he was also an extremely social creature, was often charming and gracious, had many friends, could, if he wanted to do so, sell you dubious products, and seemed to love his first wife (my mother) though she was stupid in many ways, and Rose, his second wife, who was brighter than my mother but neurotically impossible.

Henry was constantly irritable and often temper-ridden. He didn't abuse his children or hit his wife, but he often abusively screamed at them for their "stupidities"—especially when he began, while still married to Hettie, surreptitiously sleeping with Rose. He didn't seethe openly or long against his "enemies" but often exhibited low frustration tolerance (LFT) and bad moods. He wasn't exactly manic-depressive but was dysthymic. He was quite irritable, but a little later, he became forgiving.

My mother was irritable and angry for only short periods—even with my psychopathic brother and depressed and nasty sister. She took nothing, practically, *too* seriously and almost always led a cheerful, happy existence, though she worried about trivial things until she was past eighty-five. She then acquired a pessimistic outlook and was often, though not seriously, depressed.

In her heyday, when she was in her early forties, my mother was not very angry toward my father, even after she discovered he was having a secret affair with her best friend (and family devotee), Rose, a woman ten years younger than she. Nor was she angry at Rose, the real betrayer. She deplored people's *actions*—but not *them*. And she always spoke well of my father, even when he neglectfully owed her tens of thousands of dollars in alimony, which he never tried to pay. In these and other ways, she was, shall we say, unusually unangry, neglectful, and into the present, pleasant moment.

My father, however, was quite different. In some respects I take after my father. Not, I am fairly sure, because of modeling or of his teaching. He wasn't around that much, when I was a child, to model after. Often, he was away on business trips for several weeks at a time. When home, we three children saw him at 8:30 AM, to kiss him good morning—and then, usually, the next morning at 8:30 again. He was away at business—maybe monkey business!—just about every evening; on Saturday evening he went out till late with my mother; and on Sundays he had either business deals or pinochle or poker games all day with his male friends. My mother, maybe for practical reasons, put up with his absence and neglect with remarkably little complaining. She was busy, first with her children, later with her many friends, with bridge, and with Tremont Temple—no, not really the temple, but its convivial sisterhood.

I quickly got used to my father's absences and, if anything, tried to model myself around my mother's sociability. I knew she was right about not taking people (including her children) *too* seriously, and about swiftly forgiving their flaws. I appreciated her small lectures when I acted badly, and thought that I and everyone else should follow them. But, unlike her, I was often exceptionally (and instantaneously) irritable if something went wrong, or stupidly, or unfairly. By all rights, things *shouldn't* go that way. I felt that and said that. But like my mother—and quite unlike my angry and depressed sister—I rarely *dwelled* on my pain and people's wrongly causing it. I soon forgot it—till the next time.

I was very irritable about rotten *happenings* but not extremely angry at people who made them happen. Like my mother and not like my father, these feelings lasted only *briefly*. Except for my "let's change the damned world!" view, which started when I was about twelve—largely as a result of reading Upton Sinclair, Bertrand Russell, H. G. Wells, and many other reformers. They clearly realized rampant social injustices and wrote vehemently against them—helping make me a social and political revolutionist (in theory, but not yet in practice).

Why? Who *really* knows? But I have thought for a while that my irritable, rebellious, and angry tendencies are, to be sure, aided by liberal thinkers and by "terrible" injustices—but, definitely, also from hereditary influences, mainly from my father's side of the family.

One important piece of evidence. I have been a pacifist since my early days, then from the age of nineteen to twenty-three, a *real*, violence-espousing revolutionist. Even then, because I romantically believed, like Lenin, Trotsky, and many Soviet Union leaders (but *not* like Stalin), that soon after the (well-justified) bloody revolution, the state would nicely, spontaneously "wither away." I soon saw (with Stalin's and Castro's help) that this was nonsense—so I became a strong pacifist by my twenty-fifth year. Me and His Holiness, the Dalai Lama.

When I started to do and preach REBT (from January 1955 onward), I first espoused unconditional self-acceptance (USA) for myself and others—and I almost adopted unconditional other-acceptance (UOA). Like Alfred Adler, I put social interest into REBT because I fully realized that just about all humans *choose* to live in social groups and will defeat their own goals if they have merely USA. In the *interest* of their self-protection (and life preservation), they had darned well better have *social* interest and involvement. That seems logical enough.

I am told by Heinz Ansbacher (through personal communication) that Alfred Adler and his clients usually put self-interest first and social interest a close second because self-preservation seems to be the honest motive for social preservation. Whether or not Adler believed and felt this way, I for a while did.

After using REBT with thousands of clients, I created the philosophy of UOA and began to actively teach all my clients and readers that USA integrally *goes with* UOA and had better, for successful surviving and living, be emphasized. When you have UOA, you always fully accept other *people* though hardly what they often think, feel, and do. You concretely try to help them live better and more happily. You specifically love a few of them. You try to help them respect, relate to, and sometimes love each other. You work in several ways for social, political, and economic equality and justice.

Why do I favor UOA, along with USA, so strongly? Several reasons come to mind:

1. Humans cannot survive, especially when they are infants, without concerned caretakers. To survive, they must live in a social group.
2. Even as adults, they can get by on desert islands—but usually don't. Socialization makes their lives much easier—but also harder. It *usually* is worth it.
3. If people indulge in their innate and acquired tendencies to disagree with one another, they often resort to rights, feuds, wars, and sometimes genocide.
4. So far people's access to weapons of violence have been limited to bats, knives, swords, and bullets. With increasing technology, people now can increasingly gain access to dynamite, bombs, machine guns, and nuclear weapons.
5. As technology keeps developing, more groups and individuals will have access to the worst weapons, including atomic ones. Eventually some will be able to manufacture weapons on their own.
6. Because they have strong self-preservation urges, and usually have many relatives and friends, most people

will refrain from using the worst forms of weapons even when it is possible for them to do so. Some fanatics, positive that their cause is absolutely right and that other people's is absolutely wrong, will be willing—nay, eager!—to have suicide attacks against their enemies. Many more are doing so today than a decade ago. Many more will probably do so tomorrow.

7. Fanatics have always existed and still will—for a combination of biological and social learning reasons. As the world population increases, there will be more of them. Nonfanatics are sensible enough—to curb their suicidal and homicidal urges. Fanatics are not. They can—and will—do *almost anything* to "prove" their *rights* and eradicate their opponents' *wrongs*. Yes, anything.

8. In years past, fanatics were often unable to survive outside or inside mental hospitals and prisons. Today, especially with medications, probably a much higher percentage of them do so. Again, they may do *anything*, including kill themselves and others simultaneously!

Review the above facts and you will see how dangerous are our times—and tomorrow's. One solution to potential worldwide holocausts—if indeed we can arrange it—is to effectively teach the principles and practices of UOA from infancy onward to everyone and hope like hell they will work. If all citizens of the world are convinced that they can nonviolently disagree with but not violently extirpate one another, they will presumably stop working to produce Armageddon.

I can't guarantee that long-term peace education for all people will definitely save the world. But I cannot at the moment think of a better plan; and I hopefully espouse life-long training in UOA for everyone as soon as possible!

Just to show how difficult it is to achieve UOA in action, even when you firmly believe in it and spend much of your time teaching it to others directly and indirectly, let me present a personal failure in following it. As noted earlier, I began actively teaching the philosophy of unconditional other-acceptance—and powerfully preaching it—about twenty years ago, after I first started teaching my clients and readers unconditional self-acceptance in the 1950s. Vigorous USA and REBT, from the start, have gone together. Social interest, but only partial UOA, came later. Nonetheless!—after vigorously and steadily teaching UOA for two decades, I still reasonably often fail to practice it.

A case in point: The clients in my therapy group and especially our therapists who assist me in leading the group, are instructed to come *on time*, to go in room 21 across the hall from my office, to come in my office when I call them, and to not knock on my door when they come in late. Mostly, they follow these rules, but every once in a while they (especially therapists!) come late or break other rules. I rarely upset myself about that. But sometimes I do. Recently, one of my co-therapists came late to group and forgot to bring the summary report of the last group meeting and the list of homework assignments, which co-therapists are scheduled to bring.

When I witnessed this perfidy, I angrily confronted the late therapist and burst out, "You're late! Why are you late? As I've always said, 'The only excuse for lateness is death.' What were you doing?"

I knew right away that I was wrong in having this temper

tantrum, but I kept it up for a minute longer. Later, after the group was over, I reviewed my outburst and saw that it was impelled by several Irrational Beliefs. "He should *never* be late! Never! That's stupid and unforgivable, especially since he's a therapist! If he does it once more I'll get rid of him! Out of our training program! That incompetent fool! After I've worked my ass off to train him! That incredible bastard! How *could* he do this to me!"

Even as I was later going over these irrational, musturbatory beliefs, I saw how idiotic, and against REBT theory, they were; but I partially re-reacted to seeing and feeling them. Yes, co-therapists *absolutely should not* be late to group! How *terrible* and *awful*!

My profound, but inconsistent, belief in UOA was obviously not working. It took me several more minutes to *really* calm down, resolve to apologize to my co-therapist for wrongly bawling him out in front of the group; to admit my anger to the group and apologize for it, too; and to get back to teaching UOA to everyone—and myself!

The point is that fully accepting and practicing UOA is almost against "human nature." As far as I can see, the Dalai Lama, after many years of training and practice, now has it. But I don't, only partly. Back to the drawing board!

In general, however, I am okay. I rarely anger myself against people, although I often see their "trepidations." I soon realize my rage, my part in creating it, how dysfunctional it is, what to do about decreasing it, and actually (temporarily!) minimize it. But I unsanely fall victim to my anti-UOA philosophy again and again.

So people and the world are still in for it—moronically;

and I am still trying to stop them in their dull-witted tracks. Maybe our existence on this planet, with our never-ceasing anger, fury, and rage, cannot fully continue. I'll keep stubbornly saying that we can survive with UOA.

I still think that I am more "naturally" irritable than most people. My mother told me that as an infant I was hypersensitive and overactive. My skin is prone to hives, explosive itching, and other overreactions (as was that of my father, brother, and sister). I am quite allergic (as they also were). I am easily and quickly annoyed. I am, as you can see, prone to minor ailments and sicknesses. I often have low frustration tolerance for the hassles of life, despite my realizing this and working against my LFT. But even if I acquired my LFT by reacting against my somewhat unusual amount of frustrations, I still have it. And I still keep fighting it.

Let me say a little more about my use of UOA with my clients. I wrote the following in 1972 in my chapter on "Psychotherapy without Tears" in Arthur Burton's book *Twelve Therapists*:

> When I first developed rational emotive behavior therapy, I squelched a good many of my negative feelings toward my clients; but inwardly I often felt angry at their lateness and other irresponsible behavior toward me, impatient that they did not quickly see and use the marvelous self-accepting philosophies I was vigorously trying to help them acquire, upset myself about some of the cruel ways in which they continued to treat others, and enraged at their reversion to psychoanalytic, Rogerian, and other magical and boy-scoutish outlooks which I, of course, knew were full of pernicious hogwash.

It was the second of the two most important REBT out-looks which soon began to help me mightily in this respect. The first REBT theory, which virtually all my clients are actively shown how to accept, is that humans are irretrievably human—fallible, fucked-up, and full of frailty—and that they therefore had better never damn nor devilify themselves no matter what they foolishly do. The second mainstay of REBT is that, because of this same human errancy, one had better not condemn, decry, or cast into hell any other person than oneself—no matter what he or she nastily does to you or others.

As I kept practicing rational emotive behavior psychology during the middle and late 1950s, and as I kept showing my clients how crazy they were behaving when they felt angry, resentful, hostile, revengeful, or vindictive, and how they would invariably lose out (especially in the long run) by following this kind of Jehovahistic thinking, I couldn't help stopping on many occasions and saying to myself: "Dang it! Don't *I* do the same thing, too? He says he's trying to help his wife, but he's thoroughly impatient with her. Well, aren't I, who am supposedly trying to help him, equally impatient when he comes late, doesn't do his homework, or resists me with his psychodynamic horse manure? Face it! I am often doing the same thing as he does. Now what am *I* going to do to change? Healer, heal thyself!"

The same thing happened at some of my public lectures and workshops. Some hostile questioner, especially a devotee of psychoanalysis, would try to put me on the spot and make me look foolish. Whereupon I would first flash to myself: "Idiot! How can he be so dense! Here I worked through that crap a long time ago and he still devoutly and bigotedly subscribes to it. Now let me see how I can quickly fix his wagon and make him the laughingstock of everyone in the audience." And, being witty and bright, I usually did pulverize my questioner—much to the amusement of most of my audience, and much to his own horror. Naturally, that was one of the best possible ways for me to lose friends and uninfluence people, and some of the worst enemies I have to this day I nicely made in this manner.

Immediately after my clever retorts, however, I would tend to revert to my own theory and at least inwardly recant. "Look," I would tell myself, "stop the nonsense! You supposedly teach people that no one is a bastard, not even a benighted psychoanalytic religionist; and then you do your best to blast this poor individual out of her seat and make her a laughingstock even to her best friends in the audience. What kind of tolerance is that? You show people how to deplore others' traits and not their being, but you clearly were attempting to put her down as a person. How rational-emotively sane was your own behavior?"

You can well imagine that my self-criticism—or, more accurately, criticism of my own acts—did not perform instant miracles. For quite a number of years thereafter I still could not—er, did not—resist the temptation to make my public opponents look foolish. To be honest, I still don't resist on more than a few occasions. But, as many people have said to me who have heard me speak on the same topic both a decade ago and more recently, I have significantly improved in this respect. REBT works even with its originator! I still have, and think I am strongly disposed biologically to have, much of the irritability which my father displayed for the full eighty years of his life. But as I keep working against it, and keep asking myself, "Why shouldn't benighted people think the way they do about my theories? Why are they screwballs for having a few screwy ideas? What can I learn, for my own benefit and that of my theories, from their valid and invalid objections?" I keep becoming increasingly patient and less irritable, and I gain more from objectionable objections to my views than I previously did from my angry counterblasts.

The more I practice REBT with others, the more I automatically tend to use it with myself. This is why I favor group therapy so much. In my regular weekly groups, and in the marathon weekends of rational encounter that I lead in various parts of the country every year, I train most of the group members not only to use the REBT philosophy of tolerance, scientific validation, and openness with themselves but also to actively, determinedly employ it with other group members. My theory states that if they thereby keep talking others out of their bullshit, they will automatically and unconsciously tend to talk themselves out of their own. As I write this hypothesis, I can see that it could be empirically tested. I could arrange an experimental group where a participant only tried to use REBT methods with other group members and a control group where he (or other clients who had similar disturbances) only brought up his own problems to REBT-oriented group members and never tried to help those other members with their upsets. Then I could see whether, as I hypothesize, those who only (or at least mainly) worked on other people's problems with REBT made as much emotional progress themselves as the clients who only (or mainly) brought up their own problems for discussion. Well, maybe I shall do this experiment someday (for, unfortunately, I have almost innumerable things to do for the dear old cause of REBT before I die, and exceptionally little time left in which to do them). Until that day, I still maintain the hypothesis that talking others out of their magical, self-

destroying philosophies tends to help one appreciably surrender one's own tommyrot. If anyone is the living proof of
that thesis, I think it is I.

Well, I see that I forgot about my using REBT to conquer my
anger about the many times writers have obviously plagiarized
my writings and audios, refused to give me any credit, and
unethically pretended that they made up my points themselves
or got them from ancient philosophers. Like hell they did.

A case in point is that of Wayne Dyer, who was a student of
our first Director of Training, Jon Geis, came to many of my
workshops, used REBT with his clients, and published *Your
Erroneous Zones* in 1977, on which he made several million
dollars in royalties and with which he became a renowned
public speaker—even more renowned than I.

Your Erroneous Zones, as anyone who reads it and my 1975
book, *A New Guide to Rational Living*, can see, uses many of my
ideas, gives no credit whatever to me, and cites my word, *musturbation*, only once. Moreover, when asked on television if he
copied me, he categorically replied, "No, I got some of my
ideas in *Your Erroneous Zones* from ancient philosophers."

I was advised by the Institute's lawyers—probably
wrongly—not to sue Dyer, and didn't. Was I angry at him for
giving me no credit? Practically not at all. I was of course very
disappointed in his *behavior* but not angry at *him*. My friends
and supporters all over the world still are, but not I, for a
number of reasons.

1. As I just said, I decry his actions but not him, his personality, and his being. I practice UOA.

2. I realize that, while neglecting the Institute and me, he has helped many readers and listeners by spreading some of the essences of REBT around the world. Much of his later writing does not follow REBT, but *Your Erroneous Zones* lasts and helps many people considerably.
3. The anger of professionals at Dyer has sometimes aided me and my REBT reputation—and that is all to the good. The mistake of giving credit to Dyer and not to me by many authors has probably not harmed me and REBT that much.

I was not and am not happy at Dyer, but I really liked his book *Return from Eykis*, a novel that gives a much more profound version of REBT than *Your Erroneous Zones*. When, a few years ago, he (wrongly) heard that I was angry at him and wrote to me asking about this, I explained my feelings, complimented him on *Eykis*, and said that I would be glad to see him to talk further if he were in New York. He has not come to see me since then but recommends some clients to the Institute and me. So I think he now thinks I am not hostile. My unconditional other-acceptance has once again paid off.

15.

CONDUCTING MY LIFELONG BATTLE WITH DIABETES

Although I discovered that I had renal glycosuria when I was nineteen, it didn't bother me much for years. I cut down on my sugar intake despite my compulsive addiction to it before that time. My mother was similarly addicted and was caught stealing other people's candy several times at the age of ninety-three in her nursing home!

Not I. At nineteen, I ate only a little candy and other sweets when they were offered to me and never spent a penny on them. This was quite different than how I behaved at the age of thirteen. After working from Monday to Saturday selling newspapers during the summer, and making $30 to $50 a week doing so, my brother, Paul, and I went out together every Sunday night and spent $10 on the boardwalk in Wildwood, New Jersey, on food, mostly on sweets. During the week, we both consumed a pint of Breyer's ice cream and half a cheese-cake every day. Delicious!

At nineteen, I gave up sweets. I never purchased sweets and lived with my unfulfilled urges for them. Then, at about forty, I developed boils, which seemed to result from eating too much carbohydrates, and I became much stricter about my diet—living largely on protein foods. Alas, in 1958, at the age of forty-five, I was definitely diagnosed as having type 1 insulin-dependent diabetes; and, as advised in those days, I ruthlessly cut out all sugar and most fats, and started taking insulin—at first, only seven units a day. As time went by, I increased the insulin, until I now take ten units of fast-acting insulin and fifteen units of slow-acting insulin every morning. Before eating supper, I take eight more units of fast-acting and seventeen units of slow-acting insulin, without fail!

Two rounds of insulin injections every day is not so bad, so I easily put up with them. But the rest of my diabetic regimen is a real nuisance. To keep my blood sugar consistently around 100, I test it no fewer than ten times a day with finger pricks. The hassles are remembering to test my blood, pricking my calloused fingers, and eating more food when my sugar is low and less food when it is high. I do this around the clock—even three or four times in the middle of the night. I eat small meals, also around the clock, about ten times a day. Otherwise, I can go into insulin shock, with severe hypoglycemia—and perhaps die.

Example: One day in August when I was at the American Psychological Association's Annual Convention with Janet, I somehow forgot to eat enough and around 4:30 PM went into insulin shock in the elevator of our hotel. I loudly denounced the stupidity of some of my colleagues in the presentations that day, and was told by Janet to keep quiet. I took offense at her good advice and very loudly said, "Fuck all those people listening! Let them mind their own business and go back to where they came from!" I was most resistant and Janet had a rough time getting me back to our room, where she quickly got some orange juice down my gullet, and I came out of my hypoglycemic shock in about five minutes.

An even worse time was when I was fifty-three, after I began taking insulin. I went to sleep at 11 PM—when my blood sugar was low, but I had only an inaccurate method (urine testing) to measure it. I woke at 3 AM screaming and shaking. Janet couldn't get any sugary fluid into me, called a physician who answered emergencies, and had him inject some glucose into my vein. Saved again!

One more serious time. In 1972, when Janet was away from the Institute taking the internship for her PhD in psychology at NYU, hypoglycemia struck again. I related the incident in "Psychotherapy without Tears,"

> One morning, I rose an hour earlier than usual and foolishly took my regular dose of insulin immediately. Perhaps because I was sleepier and more bleary-eyed than I generally am in the morning, I probably misread the syringe markings and took five or ten extra units. I called one of our secretaries to my office when he entered the building at eight-fifty, gave him some things to do, and that is all I remember until I woke, an hour and a half later, in nearby Lenox Hill Hospital's emergency ward, dreaming that I was getting a blood transfusion and that I was in danger of dying because the

nurse in charge had left me alone and might not come back in time to save me from an overdose of infused blood. After waking, I discovered that I had gone into an insulin coma while talking to the secretary. He (not knowing what was wrong with me and thinking I had gone pretty crazy because I was acting quite irrationally) had delayed in getting help. By the time other people at our Institute had realized what was going on and got a nearby physician, I was incapable of imbibing any sugary liquids. An ambulance had to be called to take me to the hospital. At the hospital, they gave me dextrose intravenously, and I came out of the coma.

At point C, or what is called the emotional Consequence, I felt (at least momentarily) some inappropriate or dysfunctional responses directly related to the Activating Events at A. They were: (1) feelings of panic at awaking in the hospital, feeling perfectly all right physically, not remembering any of the events leading up to my being in a hospital, and wondering why the hell I was there (in a restraining bed, no less, with firm bars imprisoning me in the bed); (2) A little later, when I realized I had taken an overdose of insulin and not warned our new office people about my diabetic condition, feelings of shame because I had acted so stupidly; (3) Feelings of some anger toward the secretary who had acted stupidly when he saw I was acting bizarrely and had not immediately realized that there was something physically wrong with me and that medical attention was quickly required.

Now, according to REBT theory, the noxious Activating Events that occurred to me, at A, could not have by themselves caused my disturbed feelings or emotional Consequences at C. Instead, my Beliefs, at B, about the Activities, at A, partly caused C. What, therefore, were these Beliefs?

First, I obviously had a set of Rational Beliefs (RBs)

about A. In regard to my panic at awaking in the hospital, I first believed: "How puzzling! What am I doing here? How annoying to be in a hospital bed, with bars up its side, and not know what happened to get me here! I wish to hell I could understand this! How painful to be so confused and in doubt! Maybe there's really something wrong with me. And how unfortunate that would be!" If I had stuck rigorously to these Rational Beliefs, I presumably would have felt the highly appropriate emotions of frustration, annoyance, puzzlement, concern, and displeasure, but not panic. What, then, created the panic?

Obviously, according to REBT theory, my additional set of Irrational Beliefs (IBs). Probably: "How awful! Here I am in a hospital and have no idea why I am here or what is wrong with me. Suppose it is serious? Suppose they don't let me out? Suppose I have gone nutty, or something like that, not to remember at all what happened to me or why I am here? How horrible that would be! I couldn't stand it! My, what a weak and incompetent person I'd prove to be if I kept on being confused and puzzled like this and never got over it!"

In regard to my feelings of shame about acting stupidly about the overdose of insulin and not notifying our office people about my diabetic condition, I again had a set of Rational Beliefs: "What a stupid thing to do! How unfortunate! I certainly don't like behaving so idiotically, and I'd better watch these kinds of things next time." These Rational Beliefs, had I stayed with them, would have again made me feel frustrated, annoyed, concerned, and displeased, but not panicked.

My shame almost certainly resulted from a set of Irrational Beliefs: "What a total idiot I am! I should have acted more intelligently about the insulin and notify our employees about my diabetic condition. I really deserve to suffer for behaving so asininely! Maybe I'm such a nincompoop that I'll always keep acting like this, and that would be awful!"

My anger at the secretary who found me in the state of insulin shock arose because I originally had a set of Rational Beliefs, probably along these lines: "Shit! Isn't it too bad that he didn't act more observantly and intelligently! How unpleasant to have him make a stupid diagnostic error like that! I wish he had behaved more perspicaciously." Again, had I believed only these sane thoughts, I would have felt appropriately frustrated, annoyed, concerned, and displeased, but not angry.

I almost certainly went on, however, to a set of highly insane or Irrational Beliefs (IBs): "What a dolt he is! How could he have behaved so stupidly! He shouldn't have been so careless at jumping to wrong conclusions! How horrible it is for me to be afflicted with stupid people such as he!"

Fortunately, having worked through such Irrational Beliefs many many times with my clients and myself, I automatically went to work on my own in this instance and vigorously Disputed them, at point D. Thus, I challenged:

"Why is it awful to be in the hospital and not know what is wrong with me? Even if I have acted bizarrely, to get myself here, and I am off my rocker, where is the evidence that that is horrible?" And I quickly answered myself: "It's clearly not awful, but only inconvenient, to be here. I'll soon find out what's wrong with me. And if it is serious, it is. Tough!" So I almost immediately lost my panic and merely felt puzzled and concerned.

"What makes me a total idiot, just because I screwed up (for the first time in about seventeen years) on my insulin dose? Why should I have acted more intelligently about this and about notifying our employees about my diabetic condition? In what way would it be awful even if I kept making mistakes like this and eventually foolishly killed myself?" And I replied to myself: "Obviously, *I* am not a total idiot just because I did two foolish things. There's no reason why I *should, ought,* or *must* act more intelligently, even though it would be better if I did. It's not awful, but merely quite unpleasant, if I keep making mistakes like this and even finally kill myself by them." Whereupon I lost all my feelings of shame and considered the objective problem of how I would act more intelligently in the future and not repeat these silly errors.

"Why is our secretary a dolt just because he diagnosed my condition wrongly? Why could he not, or for that matter why could not any other human being, behave so stupidly? Where is the evidence that he should not have been so careless? What makes it horrible for me to be afflicted with fallible human beings in our office?" I directly answered these questions: "Of course, he's not a dolt just because he did one mistaken act. He easily could behave wrongly in this instance, and there is no reason why he shouldn't. It's certainly troublesome for me to be afflicted with fallible human employees; but I can still refuse to make myself childishly angry and miserable because of that difficulty." Within literally a few seconds, I lost all my anger at our secretary and, in fact, I felt grateful to him for doing as much as he was able to do for me when I was in insulin shock and for at least calling in others who better knew what to do.

After the entire experience was over, and I had rid myself, by prompt use of REBT methods, of my feelings of panic, shame, and hostility, I actually felt fine about the events of the day. For I thought as follows: "It certainly was a damned nuisance to go into shock, to inconvenience and help stir up the negative emotions of so many people. But this sort of thing has never happened to me before, and it was a fascinating and interesting experience. In fact, in some ways I'm happy it occurred, since it adds to my repertoire of intriguing things that have happened to me and that I can remember and learn from. Moreover, now that I've almost killed myself with my careless behavior, I can profit from my experience and rarely let it happen again. You know, I'm rather glad that it, or at least certain aspects of it, happened."

Another more serious incident of insulin shock occurred when I was in Ontario, Canada, the night I was to give a public talk on REBT to more than three hundred people and then an all-day workshop for professionals. On the plane to Ontario I saw that I was becoming shaky, got some extra orange juice, and seemed to be fine. But in my hotel, waiting to be taken to dinner, I fell asleep—and woke up in shock in the hospital.

I learned something important from the hospital doctor who injected me with dextrose and got me back to quick consciousness: Orange juice—and similar fluids—can stave off insulin shock but, unless one also takes solid food with them, they may quickly rebound and send you into greater shock. I had taken the juice and went, only an hour after I took it, into severe shock. Since then, I eat more solidly when I suspect that shock is incipient.

My hosts in Ontario were quite upset, called off my talk that night, and took me to (a solid) dinner. I protested that, one hour before the lecture was to begin, I was back in fine shape and could easily give it. No dice—it was called off, and I merely gave my professional workshop, being in great shape, the next day.

Since that time, more than thirty years ago, I have carefully watched my insulin taking, blood testing, and eating ten times a day, and had a few near-shock times, and never ended up in the hospital.

My reaction to those experiences? Excellent. Since the incident in 1972, when I was fifty-nine, I have taught myself to be unashamed of having diabetes, mistakenly letting my blood sugar go too low, waking up in the hospital, disappointing hundreds of people at a lecture, and other ways of bothering people with my diabetic problems. I feel sorry and disappointed about bothering people, but never embarrassed or humiliated.

Here is a good example: I often am on a speaking panel with several other people, appearing before a large audience. I arrive early, with my blood tester, food, sucrose tablets, orange juice, and sometimes with my insulin and needle. I wait for my time to talk, and till that time, in full view of the audience, I often test my blood, eat a sandwich, and take some juice or a sucrose tablet. Sometimes, I give myself an insulin shot—also in view of the audience. No shame, despite some of the startled looks I receive.

One time, while being interviewed by a reporter at a conference I was attending, I stopped to eat and tend to my sugar level during our talk and I was amused to see his later newspaper report: "Dr. Ellis was so rushed by giving several papers to the convention the day I interviewed him for this article that he had no time to eat all day, and had to interrupt our interview to gulp down a sandwich." The reporter didn't bother to find out that, presentations or not to give, I (on time!) had my usual meals that day. I preferably should have explained my eating habits to him, and offered him a bite of my sandwich!

Shame: what is its essence? Eleanor Roosevelt said it is "Taking your self-downing by others and making it your own." In regard to my major health problem, my diabetes, I *now* am remarkably unashamed.

16.

COPING WITH
MY PARENTS' DIVORCE

I have no serious objections to divorcing one's mate, partly because my parents were divorced and ultimately made so little of their separation. At first, they were ashamed—at least my mother was. She kept it a secret while the divorce was in process. I discovered it one summer when I was twelve and she told my aunt Fanny about it, thinking that I was asleep and couldn't hear her. After it actually occurred, a year later, she seemed to fully accept it and had no trouble telling people she was divorced.

Maybe she accepted the divorce because she was entirely faultless in her and my father's marriage, was completely faithful, and bore three children to him within five years of marriage. Henry, culprit that he was, probably had several affairs during the twelve years of their marriage (and before, when they dated for ten years!). He finally was caught sharing a roomette with Rose, my mother's best friend, on the famous 20th Century train from New York to Chicago. As usual, he had chutzpah.

He immediately moved to another apartment (in Manhattan) and divorce proceedings began. I knew something was wrong because, in addition to his moving, I stopped off with my mother to visit a lawyer's office in Philadelphia and wasn't told her reasons for the hour-long visit, but I suspected.

When I heard, while the divorce was in progress, that it was going to occur, I wasn't too shocked. Don't forget that my father often was away on long trips from the start of the marriage and on short trips when he regularly lived at home. So we were all *used* to his absence, not to mention his letting my mother always "rule." The times when he suggested or told me and my sister and brother what to do were rare. I hardly remember them. We got along very well without him—and mainly did our own thing. We generally followed our mother's rules—such as they were—and didn't miss our father's suggestions. Therefore, his separating from living with us made little difference.

After our parents' divorce my mother and us children continued to live in our apartment in the Bronx—mainly at 183rd Street and Andrews Avenue. He visited us about once a year, and at first we never visited his (and Rose's) apartment on West End Avenue in Manhattan. We rarely talked on the phone as I recall. Later on, my brother and I had a (gorgeous) meal cooked by Rose at his place once or twice a year, and my sister, Janet, also had a meal at his place less often.

We all took it well. We were not close but were friendly. Paul and I got by very nicely without our father and did not miss him. Janet, whom Paul and I were also not close to, also seemed to not miss him. But maybe she did.

One notable event occurred when I was about to graduate from high school at the age of sixteen and was set to go to the College of the City of New York to study business administration. My father suddenly showed up at my high school to tell me that my brother, Paul, had smallpox and that he, my mother, and my sister were all quarantined in our Bronx apartment. If I went home, I would be quarantined, too, and might miss my graduation. He was therefore taking me to get a room at the Empire Hotel at Broadway and 65th Street, a block away from my High School of Commerce, and to arrange for me to stay there for a month or so—until my family was no longer quarantined and I could live at home again.

My father took me to the Empire Hotel, paid the bill for a month, and I had a nice room there to stay in alone. It was quite a break! Previously, I had been away from home only during my hospital stays—and I then had many nurses and doctors to take care of me and other children all around me. Now I was really and truly to live alone. It was a different experience for a sixteen-year-old homebody!

As you may expect, I again took it well. My father gave me $50—for food and incidentals for the first week—which I thought was a generous sum; and from that night on, I was on my own: no one to provide food, no brother to talk to, no mother to take care of things, none of my things except a few school books and a typewriter.

I thanked my father for everything. He had gone far out of his way to leave business that day and take care of me. I appreciated it and had a long, and almost close, talk with him. After dinner with him, I had no plans, and only a small room with four walls. Almost desolate.

I decided to make the most of it, and planned what to do. I would particularly go to the nearby Broadway movies and see the first-run musicals that I doted upon. That very night I saw the first one—I think *The Vagabond King* with Rudolf Friml's outstanding music. Then for the next thirty days I took in thirty other movies, mostly musicals. Thirty movies—night after night and some during the day. Wow!

This led to my starting a new hobby, which I continued the rest of my life—composing words and music of "sensible" songs. I had been devoted to semi-classical and classical music all my life—my mother tells me since I kept singing at the age of two in the cradle. I had no real musical training, but I could whistle like hell and create variations on old tunes and scores of original ones as I walked along the street or lay on the sofa in our apartment. I *knew* they were good and that I would one of these days be a brilliant light-opera composer.

This month away from home, being unable to do many things I routinely did, I added the composition of lyrics to my songs. I instantly, without effort, whistled my tunes, but writing song lyrics took more time and effort—which I had and was grateful to use. So I wrote several complete songs in my month in Manhattan—and have kept at it ever since.

My song lyrics were designed to be different—sensibly or rationally different. None of that June-moon stuff for me. I took my own tunes and some from the masters and wrote lyrics for them that were deliberately not silly, super-romantic drivel. I thought I would start a revolutionary style—and, again, become famous and make more money than Irving

Berlin. I'll tell you later what happened, when I finish writing my autobiography.

Meanwhile, I was too damned busy—going to movies and writing my songs—to be very miserable about my month of loneliness. I had time to think for myself and muse about the unusual life that was happening to me. So I mused that it had real disadvantages—and also advantages. For example, I had money to spend, entertainments, time to think for myself, time to read voraciously, and no one to bother me. I decided to enjoy all this and not demand more. I implemented my decisions.

I felt sad, particularly to miss my nightly talks with Paul about his adventures with girls and my lack of adventures. But I was not too sad about my aloneness. I had often, before, made myself focus on the advantages of being pained—like seeing and talking to the pretty nurses when I was confined in the hospital. Now I did more of that than before—especially since I had the joy of my new songwriting.

People—as I see with my clients—emphasize their trouble so awfulizingly that they can hardly think about or enjoy their concomitant pleasures and gains. At the age of sixteen, I began to focus on the doughnut rather than the hole in it. I was about to become a "real" philosopher during the next year. Musingly, I was already on the way!

17.

How I Used My Social Failings to Become a "Real" Philosopher

I didn't, as I relate elsewhere in this book, get over my fear of failing with women till I was almost twenty. From thirteen to sixteen I went to an all-boys school, the High School of Commerce, and that didn't help very much. I also lived in a new neighborhood, 183rd Street and Andrews Avenue, that had few kids my age and therefore I had few neighborhood friends.

Mainly, however, I chose not to have many friends. It was largely out of fear, since I didn't have a younger group of boys to play with and favor because they were as poor at sports as I was. So I avoided the same-age boys on Andrews Avenue who would have shown me up at sports, and mainly played street tennis with Paul (whom I accepted as a better player than I).

As for girls, there were few in my neighborhood, but I avoided them because I was *so* horny for all of them and didn't really know how to talk to them. My one best bet was a bright girl who had been in my junior high school class, with whom I flirted, but I deemed too respectable to approach. She lived in the corner, high-class apartment house on University Avenue, and her father was a well-to-do physician. My parents had just divorced and we were relatively poor, with my wearing cut-down jackets from my much bigger father. So, typical of me, I fearfully avoided talking to this doctor's daughter when we passed on the street. She was too high class and attractive for me!

I stayed by myself after school, played with my brother, and had a very active life writing stories—and now I also collected song lyrics to hit tunes, and became devoted to The Biggest News of the Week Contest, run by the *New York World*, and for which I and my high school won many prizes.

When I was soon to be sixteen, one of my old friends invited me to his birthday party, and I hesitatingly went, since parties (with girls present!) were again not my thing. We had a few dances at high school, where we boys danced with each other but not with girls—except at the senior prom, which I did not attend because I had no girl to invite to it. My mother, who adored dancing, said that she would be my date, but I thought that inappropriate.

I went to Mort's birthday party partly in fear and found that almost all the kids were a year older than I (as Mort was) and already a year into college. Being afraid of the (ravishingly beautiful and big-titted) girls, I spoke with a group of bright boys, particularly with Sid, who was into philosophy. He was discussing it enthusiastically, said that he had already decided to be a philosophy professor, and urged me (and all the others present) to follow him.

I could see right away that although I was unusually well read—more, probably, than any of the other boys—I knew virtually nothing about Kant, Schopenhauer, Nietzsche, and other philosophers that Sid was enthusiastic about. I was sadly ignorant—and silent!—about them. Shit! I was a great literateur—but a dull, dingy clod as a philosopher. And philosophy, as Sid kept pointing out, was the summit of summits.

I was thoroughly ashamed of myself for my great lapse at the age of sixteen. I had conquered some sex shame and other shame at this time, but not this *intellectual* shame. After all, I surmounted my lack of skill at sports, socializing, and science, as well as other *mental* pursuits. I was fully acknowledged by my (bright) friends, by teachers, and by adults. Now all this hardly counted. I was *philosophically* disgraced.

I instantly knew what to do: discontinue my failing sports and womanizing life—to hell with all that!—and make myself into an authoritative, outstanding philosopher. Indeed, maybe a *professor* of philosophy, as Sid was sure he would be.

This decision was somewhat ironic. At the moment, I was enrolled in a bachelor of business administration program at City College of New York. I had conferred with my father and his accountant months before and decided that at this time, with the Great Depression of 1929 about to occur, I could write all I wanted, but I had to make sure I had a safe profession. I would be an accountant, or at least a teacher of accounting, and make a good living. In fact, my father's accountant promised me a job in his firm—the notable accounting firm of Price & Waterhouse—as soon as I finished my degree. Besides, I already knew from high school that I was unusually good at accounting.

I wasn't about to abandon my schooling plans. I happily entered the High School of Commerce for the next three years—where I did marvelously and then went on to my BBA degree. But I *really*, from sixteen onward, was a closet philosopher. Using three library privileges—the New York Public Library, the Mercantile Library on 43rd Street, and the Russell Sage Library, a block from my college (on 23rd Street), I devoured practically every classical philosophy book during my high school years. I included psychology and sociology, and I continued to read literature. But in my high school and college days I became something of an authority on ancient Asian, ancient Greek and Roman, and modern eighteenth- to twentieth-century European philosophy. I really went at it in full—and perhaps put to shame Sid and everyone else.

I confess that I did it partly for the prestige. Philosophy seemed to be much deeper and more profound than other approaches and so it really got to the most important. Or, after I became a great philosopher, I would make it get to the most important.

After favoring philosophy at the age of sixteen, I incorporated it in my practice of psychotherapy and REBT, as shown in the following excerpt from an interview I had in 2000, with Robert Epstein, the editor of *Psychology Today*.

> Albert Ellis is a force to be reckoned with, both as a person and as a professional. Renowned as much for his colorful language and strong opinions as for his innovations in therapy, Ellis developed what is now called "Rational Emotive Behavior Therapy" (REBT) in the mid-1950s. The groundbreaking therapy is based on his main philosophy: that most of our behavioral and emotional problems—from

getting over a breakup to handling child abuse—stem from our own irrational beliefs about our situations and how we should be treated. Quickly and powerfully, REBT helps you replace such irrational thoughts with rational ones. Given that these techniques have now become mainstream, it's safe to say that no individual—not even Freud himself—has had a greater impact on modern psychotherapy. At 87, Ellis still lectures, writes and sees 70 or more clients per week—his steady stream of gusto and bravado apparently unstoppable.

RE: You are widely known as a very unusual person—as a kind of character. Do you agree?

AE: Yes, compared to most therapists, and probably to the general population, because I usually tell it like it is. And I don't give that much of a damn what people think of me for saying it. That's unusual, since the world consists mainly of love slobs who need other people's approval. Most people don't live their own lives very well.

RE: How long have you spoken your mind?

AE: A long time. I majored in business administration in college, but my hobby was philosophy and I read all the philosophers. When I was 16 I started keeping a diary in which I recorded my disagreements with the famous philosophers.

RE: Could this be interpreted as a kind of arrogance?

AE: Yes, but I didn't insist that they were wrong, that I was right and I had to prevail. I just agreed and disagreed with them. I thought there was a high degree of probability that I was right and some other thinkers were wrong. But I wasn't positive about it.

RE: Has speaking your mind ever gotten you in trouble?

AE: Yes, several times. For example I wrote a book with a psychiatrist, and I did practically all the work. It was a study of sex offenders in the New Jersey State system, where I was chief psychologist. I started to get it published and put his name second—it's dubious whether he even deserved that—and he got angry and complained to the famous Sanford Bates, then director of the Department of Human Services. Bates said I had to put the psychiatrist's name first. I held my ground and practically got kicked out of the state of New Jersey. I ended up quitting and going into private practice in 1952.

RE: How did you feel about that?

AE: I felt that I was right and they were wrong, but I wasn't upset, even though the process was very unfair. They trumped up charges, for example, that I lived in New York and shouldn't be allowed to work for the state of New Jersey. I pointed out that half the people working for the state lived in Philadelphia. But I don't recall that I was terribly angry at them. I just noted that they were unfair.

RE: Nevertheless, you paid a price for your boldness. Isn't that the reason most people won't speak their minds?

AE: Yes, and I don't recommend that people speak their minds to their bosses or to somebody who's directly over them. You'd better know when to speak your mind and what the penalty will be for doing so. Sometimes it's worth it, and often it's not!

RE: You were trained initially in the Rogerian tradition of therapy, which is entirely nondirective. Then you shifted to Freudian psychoanalysis. How did you end up developing your very own directive technique?

AE: I was trained in Rogerian therapy at Columbia University, but I didn't buy it so I never practiced it. I had used eclectic therapy and behavior therapy on myself at the age of 19 to get over my fear of public speaking and my terror of approaching young women in public. So I used other forms of therapy on myself, and I started to use those with clients. But I thought foolishly that Freudian psychoanalysis was deeper and more intensive than other, more directive forms of other therapy, so I was trained in it and practiced it. Then I found that it intensively went into every irrelevancy under the sun—and that it didn't work. People got insights into what was bothering them, but they hardly did a damn thing to change. Freud had a gene for inefficiency, and I think I have a gene for efficiency. Had I not been a therapist, I would have been an efficiency expert.

RE: Freudian therapists do a lot of listening and very little persuading.

AE: Right, and that was one of the reasons I eventually gave up being an analyst. I wrote several articles criticizing psychoanalysis after practicing it for six years.

RE: You made this shift, as I recall, around 1955. Some time during this transitional period you began to focus on a very critical idea—namely, that our problems are rooted in irrational beliefs. How did this idea merge?

AE: When I started to get disillusioned with psychoanalysis I reread philosophy and was reminded of the constructivist notion that Epictetus had proposed 2,000 years ago: "People are disturbed not by events that happen to them, but by their view of them." I could see how that applied to many of my clients. One was a very shy man whose father had taken him out at the age of 4 and made him shoot at birds and animals with a great big shot gun. He really loathed himself in many respects. When I showed him that he had underlying irrational thoughts that led to negative feelings about himself, he denied it, and also denied that he hated his father. But one time I probed and probed and suggested that it was what he told himself that upset him. And he finally admitted, "Damn it. I really do hate him. I could kill him right now because he shouldn't have done what he did when I was a little boy and made me so afraid of people and things." I saw—and *he* saw—that it wasn't just his father's behavior, what I call "adversity" that made him angry and self-doubting. It was also his "belief system," what he told himself about the adversity.

RE: How did he turn out?

AE: He didn't completely get over his shyness, but he saw that his father had serious problems of his own. He was able to accept disliking his father and to get along with him. I also had a great many sex and love cases where people were absolutely devastated when somebody with whom they were compulsively in love didn't love them back. They were killing themselves with anxiety and depression. They were telling themselves, "I absolutely *must* be loved by the person I love or I am no good as a person." And I started pointing out their irrational demands and disputing their shoulds and musts, and some of them got remarkably better quite quickly.

RE: What's an irrational belief, and how can it interfere with our normal functioning?

AE: If something is irrational, that means it won't work. It's usually unrealistic. People are terrified of other people or difficult projects because they tell themselves that they could fail or be rejected. Failure can lead to sorrow, regret, frustration and annoyance—all healthy, negative feelings without which people couldn't exist. But then they add, "I absolutely *must* succeed and *must* be loved." My rational emotive behavior therapy (REBT) was one of the few therapies that was originated partly or largely because I wanted to be brief and efficient. And therefore right from the start I was active and directive. I tried to show people their musturbatory philosophy and how to work at changing it cognitively, emotionally, and behaviorally.

RE: How did REBT develop?

AE: I started to call myself a "Rational Therapist" in January 1955; later I used the term "rational emotive." Now I call myself a "rational emotive behavior therapist." But from the start, I always included philosophical techniques as well as experiential, emotional and behavioral techniques. At first I did REBT myself. Then I taught it to a few of my friends who were psychotherapists. And then I began in 1956 to start teaching it to others. In 1959 I got a great big Ampex tape recorder and recorded specific sessions that I had with my clients and started sending samples to other therapists. That year I also established the Institute for Rational Living, which later became the Institute for Rational Emotive Therapy and then the Albert Ellis Institute, which trains therapists and gives them certificates in REBT.

RE: How did the profession react to REBT?

AE: I was ostracized by most of the psychological, psychiatric and social work professions. Therapists said REBT was superficial. It won't work. They wrongly said it has no "feeling" aspects. Some said it wasn't behavioral, although it was very behavioral. Critics said all kinds of things about it and objected philosophically and otherwise to it. But essentially they said it wouldn't work.

RE: Who were the most vocal critics?

AE: One was Fritz Perls. Whenever we were on a symposium together he would say, "I'm bored. It's too rational. It has no feeling." Many psychoanalysts refused to let me speak at their meetings. They were exceptionally vigorous because I had previously been an analyst and they were very angry at my flying the coop. Practically every other kind of therapist was opposed to REBT.

RE: You and the thousands of therapists you've trained and influenced have used REBT with perhaps millions of people. What evidence do you have that it works?

AE: In my very first paper on what we now call REBT, I outlined 11 common irrational beliefs. Later I added 30 or 40 more common irrational ideas. Beginning in the 1960s, many studies showed that people who hold what we call irrational beliefs are significantly more disturbed than when they don't hold them, and the more strongly they hold them, the more disturbed they tend to be. We started doing outcome studies, and then later on Aaron Beck and Donald Meichenbaum began to do them, and now there are probably 2,000 or more studies on the effectiveness of Cognitive Behavior Therapy, which I originated. The studies tend to show that when people change their irrational beliefs to undogmatic flexible preferences, they become less disturbed.

RE: Are there any particular populations that are more resistant to this technique?

AE: The psychotics, naturally. They don't think straight. And severe personality disorders take much longer to treat than people who are neurotic.

RE: A classic joke on the passivity of Cognitive Behavior Therapy goes as follows: A client tells Carl Rogers, the quintessential nondirective therapist, that she feels like committing suicide. Rogers replies, "You're feeling suicidal." She says, "Yes, I feel like jumping out the window," and Rogers replies, "You feel like jumping out the window." She walks over to the window, and Rogers follows. She jumps, and Rogers leans out the window and says, "Plop." Could this happen with your own therapeutic approach?

AE: No, because we'd immediately say, "What are you telling yourself to make yourself suicidal? You largely constructed your depression. It wasn't given to you. Therefore, you can deconstruct it. What do you think you're telling yourself to make yourself this way?" We'd get the client to admit things like, "I don't like my life" and then we'd say, "Yeah, but that wouldn't induce you to commit suicide. What else are you telling yourself?" And that's when clients would say things like, "It shouldn't be the way it is. It's terrible that I failed. I'm no good." That's when we hear the shoulds, the oughts and the musts, and then we convince the client to abandon these irrational demands. Our slogan is, "I will not *should* on myself today."

RE: Rogers' approach and your approach seem to be miles apart.

AE: But they're also similar in one respect. We both had the idea—which I think we both got from Paul Tillich's book *The Courage to Be*—that humans can accept themselves unconditionally. But Rogers thought he could get people to accept themselves just by listening to them and being nice to them, and I don't think that's enough. I think nine out of ten people who go through Rogerian therapy conclude wrongly that "I'm okay because my therapist approves of me." But that's conditional love. I get people to truly accept themselves unconditionally, whether or not their therapist or anyone loves them. Self-esteem is the greatest sickness known to man or woman because it's conditional. "When I do well and am loved by significant others, then I'm okay." Rogers would have been opposed to that as an endpoint to therapy, but he didn't have a good technique for showing people how to get beyond it. In REBT, we give clients unconditional acceptance but we also teach them how to give it to themselves.

RE: Several professional organizations are now cautioning therapists that by being too directive they might inadvertently be implanting false memories in their clients. Do you worry about this?

AE: With all directive techniques including classroom teaching the teacher or therapist might indoctrinate the pupils or the clients with wrong ideas which could be harmful to them. That's a liability.

RE: Let's get more concrete about this. A man comes in and says, "I've been feeling horrible lately, and I think it's because I may have been abused as a child." How do you react?

AE: We'd assume the worst, usually as a hypothesis. Let's suppose somebody abused you sexually. You still had a choice—though not a good one—about what to tell yourself about the abuse. Given that you're still upset about the abuse, you probably told yourself two things about it. First you said things like: "I don't like it. I wish to hell it weren't so. How unfair." That made you feel sorry and regretful, which is okay. But you also in all probability told yourself that the abuse should not exist. You were disturbed as a child because of both the adversity you experienced and what you told yourself about the adversity. If adversity alone caused disturbance, then everybody who experienced such adversity would turn out the same, but we know they don't. So we teach people that they upset themselves then and that they're still doing it now. We can't change the past, so we change how people are thinking, feeling and behaving today.

RE: By assuming that the abuse really occurred, isn't there a danger here that you might inadvertently implant a memory?

AE: No, because after we show people that they are partly responsible for their upsetness, then we say, "Now that you're not very disturbed about it, what were the details? Did it really occur?"

RE: So you're basically helping people to protect themselves from the worst case.

AE: Right. That's what we call the "elegant solution." You might say that your wife is nasty and mean and blames you for everything. You say that makes you angry. We'll assume that she really behaves this way and teach you how to get unangry. Then you can decide whether she was really that bad.

RE: How old are you?

AE: I'm close to 90.

RE: And how many clients do you see?

AE: When I'm in New York, I see about 40 individual clients, and I also have four groups with eight people apiece. So I see as many as 70 or more clients per week.

RE: What does it cost to have therapy with Albert Ellis?

AE: We're a nonprofit organization, and it usually costs $100 an hour for individual therapy. Participating in a group costs $120 a month.

RE: That seems like quite a value, considering that some of my therapist friends consider you to be the greatest living therapist in the world. Are you?

AE: Well, in terms of my personal effectiveness with clients, I think that I'm certainly one of the most effective therapists doing REBT or cognitive behavior therapy. Whether I'm the best in the world—that would certainly be questionable with so many therapists around.

RE: Do you think the Freudian tradition will ever die?

AE: It will never completely die because it has a few good points. For example, people have motives and thoughts of which they are unaware. Most of cognitive therapy has now adopted a similar idea. On the other hand, the relationship part of psychoanalysis where you must have a deep, emotional relationship with the client—will, I think, get kicked in the teeth one of these days. I just had a client this week who came to me after ten years of Freudian therapy. He's in love with his analyst, and she is sort of in love with him, though she's not going to bed with him. There's no question that she has aided this kind of intense personal involvement.

RE: Freudians call this transference and countertransference, of course. Does this also happen in REBT?

AE: Oh yes, and I recently wrote an article on it. In one situation, I was going too easy on a client because she was very bright and attractive. I didn't get after her about her low frustration tolerance, which I might have done with some other client or with a male client. She took me to task for it, and she was right, I was too taken with her. But I watch that, to see that it doesn't interfere with therapy.

RE: Are you married? Any children?

AE: I lived "in sin" with the executive director of the Institute for 37 years. I was married twice, briefly, before that.

RE: Any children?

AE: None to speak of.

RE: Any regrets about that?

AE: I would have liked having children to some degree but frankly I haven't got the time to take the kids to the goddamn ball game. So it would have been more disadvantagous than advantagous for them.

RE: Do you think it's irrational for people to say "I don't want to be in a relationship"?

AE: It could be rational or irrational. It's irrational when it's defensive because they're really afraid of rejection. But they could rationally decide that prolonged relationships take up too much time and effort and that they'd much rather do other kinds of things. But most people are afraid of rejection.

RE: You appear to be unflappable. Is there anything I could say that would upset you?

AE: I doubt it. As a matter of fact, as a result of my philosophy, I wasn't even upset about Hitler. I was willing to go to war to knock him off, but I didn't hate him. I hated what he was doing.

RE: Your philosophy is not just something you teach; it is something you live by.

AE: I hope so.

RE: You're an unusually accomplished person.

AE: Very few people have written more than 70 books and 800 papers—I've lost count.

RE: Are you also happy?

AE: Oh yes, I'm very happy. I like my work and I like various aspects of it—going around the world, teaching the gospel according to St. Albert. I like that. And seeing clients, doing group therapy, writing books.

RE: So now we get to the critical question: Are you productive and successful and happy *because* of your philosophy?

AE: To some degree yes, because most people would have given up when faced with all the criticism I've received over the years. I'm one of the best-loved psychologists in the United States, but I'm also probably the most hated one, now that Fred Skinner has died. I even wrote a paper years ago showing why we were both so productive. It was because we both didn't give much of a damn what other people thought of us. So by not caring too much about what people think, I'm able to think for myself and propagate ideas which are very often unpopular. And I succeed with them because, again, I don't care too much what other people think.

RE: Could people claim that when a client goes through this process and comes out feeling good and functioning well, he or she has become a cognitive clone of Albert Ellis?

AE: If they did we would be opposed to it. We teach people to be flexible, scientific and logical in their thinking and therefore to be less prone to brainwashing by the therapist.

RE: What would the world be like if everyone in the world thought like Albert Ellis?

AE: Oh, I think it would be a hell of a lot better. People would be largely free of neurosis. They would be much more creative and try all kinds of things that they might fail at and be rejected by others for failing at. They'd do things just because they like doing them.

RE: What would relationships be like?

AE: People would have unconditional self-acceptance. They'd always accept themselves no matter who disliked them or what they did badly. They'd also have unconditional other-acceptance. They'd always accept other people, although not necessarily what other people do, which means they would be less prejudiced or combative. They'd also have high frustration tolerance in the face of adversity.

RE: Would divorce still occur?

AE: Yes. Acceptance is not love. You love a person because he or she has lovable traits, but you accept everybody just because they're alive and human.

RE: What would psychology be like?

AE: I think the future of psychotherapy and psychology is in the school system. We had better teach every child how to rarely seriously disturb himself or herself and how to overcome disturbance when it occurs. In that sense, psychotherapy belongs in the schools.

RE: What do you see yourself doing over the next few years?

AE: I see myself continuing pretty much as I do now, for as long as I'm able. I'm getting more fragile. I have arthritis of the thumbs and I can't walk as well as I used to. I may have to restrict my activities, but if so I'll do more here at the Institute—give workshops here rather than traveling around the world. And I hope to die in the saddle seat.

RE: Do you have any regrets?

AE: I regret that I've been so busy with clinical work that I haven't been able to spend much time on experiments and outcome studies. Fortunately, Beck and Meichenbaum and other clinicians have done some of it. But theoretically—and especially if I had been a member of the academic establishment—I could have done other experiments which haven't been done.

RE: How do you want to be remembered?

AE: I would like to be remembered as one of the individuals who founded, ideologically and practically, cognitive behavior therapy and who pioneered multimodal or integrated therapy.

RE: Any final thoughts?

AE: People don't just get upset. They contribute to their upsetness. They always have the power to think, and to think about their thinking, which the goddamn dolphin, as far as we know, can't do. Therefore they have much greater ability to change themselves than any other animal has, and I hope that REBT teaches them how to do it.

RE: So there's hope for humanity?

AE: Yes. I think there's definite hope. But there are three musts that hold us back: "I *must* do well. Other people *must* treat me well. And the world *must* be easy." And I sometimes think that as long as we keep the second must, which is socially learned, then some screwballs 100 years from now will manufacture atomic bombs in their bathtub and maybe annihilate the whole human race because they demand that the rest of the world must agree with their dogmas. When we don't agree, they may zap us. So we better work hard on getting rid of the second must, "Other people *must* do what I want them to do!" It's what makes people hostile, nasty, mean and combative, and it leads to feuds, wars and genocide. We'd better do something about that.

18.

SUCCEEDING IN SPITE OF NEGLECT AND OPPOSITION

D r. Michael S. Broder, a pioneer in REBT, focused on my success with it, in spite of great opposition to me, and he interviewed me about this when I was in my late eighties.

Our interview follows:

MSB: Al, let's start off with the basics. I doubt if anyone could argue that in our field you are the very definition of success. When I think of all you have accomplished—not only conceptualizing cognitive behavior therapy and REBT theory and practice, but also taking your groundbreaking work from being renegade to state of the art through your countless books and articles, founding and operating the Albert Ellis Institute, which continues to grow internationally, and being considered a mentor by more psychotherapists around the world than perhaps anyone else alive—I consider those achievements monumental. I know you do, too. To what do you attribute your ability to manifest that kind of success?

AE: Well, several things, not necessarily in order. First of all, there is persistence. That is, I persist at what I do. I get an idea and I keep working at it. Get more evidence and change it and presumably improve it. So along with that persistence may be flexibility. I start with an idea and then I keep revising it. And, of course, a big thing, which many people don't do that I think is far more important, is that, I take criticism of what I'm *doing*. But if it's criticism of me personally then I don't take it too seriously.

MSB: Talk some more about that.

AE: Any innovator, like Darwin or Galileo, gets criticism. Some people are just jealous; other people think his or her ideas are crazy, for one reason or another. I probably get more criticism than most people because I do some original things. But that criticism doesn't stop me. I don't need love or approval. They are nice, but I don't think that my motive for doing most things is for approval. My motive is to be effective. Now that's the big thing with me. I try to be effective with my own projects and with the things I do for other people. The work I do with REBT and my goals and purposes are for me, but I also do it to help other people. The main thing I keep in mind is efficiency. So I change my ideas. I keep revising them to make them more efficient, even if they already seem to work. Many therapies work to some degree. But I formulated REBT because I wanted to have a therapy that, first of all, would work faster because people who come to therapy are in pain. Secondly, I tried for a therapy that would be more comprehensive and intensive, so that clients would not just *feel better*, they would also *get* better. I like efficiency. My goal as a therapist is to solve personal and social problems. I'm a problem solver. I try to figure out better solutions. As the old saying goes, necessity is the mother of invention. When you want to do something well, you try—if present techniques don't work [try] new ones. I keep going until I not only find what seems to be a solution, but a better solution. And I don't say, "This works, therefore I'll stop." I want it to work better.

As I frequently say, if I hadn't been a therapist I probably would have been some kind of efficiency expert. I'd go into an organization and try to make it work better. Because I like that. I hate inefficiency. That's partly because, again, for many years I've recognized the fact that life is short and the one thing you never get back is time. If you spend time, it's spent. You never get those hours back. It doesn't work backwards; it only works forward. So therefore I try to do most things quickly but efficiently. Not just quickly, because I could do it sloppily. It's a matter of doing it fast *and* accurately.

I also keep that in mind for my own personal life. I throw out many things that would be time consuming, even though some of them would be pleasurable. I am devoted to music but forego much of it because it would be too time consuming. I try to make the world better. So I rarely am thoroughly pessimistic, even about certain things that are really unfortunate. Like, for example, the fads in therapy. Real fads. Therapists often invent repressed memories of childhood sexual abuse that presumably cause adult disturbances. We have tons of workshops on this kind of stuff, many of which are serious distortions. So these fads interfere with a client's understanding and using rational emotive behavior therapy. They divert people from it. And I say it's too bad, but I'm not totally pessimistic, nor do I think that effective therapy will go out of business because of its fads. Unfortunately, there will be new fads and new fads that will interfere with sanity in psychotherapy. But they won't destroy it.

MSB: One of the things that I'm writing about is the whole world of intrinsic versus extrinsic rewards. As long as I've known you, almost twenty-five years, I've never seen you go for an extrinsic reward. Am I missing something?

AE: Well I think you're probably right. I go for practical rewards. If I give a good workshop, I may help a good many people and make some income for the Institute. So that's practical.

MSB: Do you see the Institute as something that will go on way beyond you?

AE: Yes.

MSB: The thing that motivates you is obviously intrinsic, but can you put your finger on just what that is? In other words, when you look at the Institute, the stuff you've written, the stuff you've done, the people who follow you, the books that are written by you and all that, selfishly speaking what's in it for you?

AE: My basic goals are to push REBT, and to improve it so as to help more people use it. So those are my goals. And when my goals are successful, I like it because they are *my* goals. They are somewhat extrinsic because I want REBT to be successful in the world. That I like. I think that REBT and cognitive behavior therapy (CBT) will help more people more of the time in an efficient manner than other therapies. That's great!

MSB: So when you think of your reward, you basically think of your contribution on a spiritual level kind of thing?

AE: Yes, spiritual in the sense that it is purposive and helpful to humanity. My contributions fulfill my purposes of efficiently helping troubled people, therapists' purpose of enhancing this help, and clients' and readers' purposes of helping themselves. This kind of abetting meaningful human goals may be called, if you will, spiritual. I sometimes call it rational spirituality!

MSB: Is there anything that you in retrospect would have done differently?

AE: Well, yes, I made a real error in allowing our research to be done by other people. Now Aaron Beck has done very well by showing that cognitive therapy works in practice. We have done similar research, but by no means enough. If I were to do it over again, I would do much more outcome research in REBT.

MSB: You mentioned Beck. Does it bother you that he doesn't really acknowledge your contribution to his work?

AE: Well, yes. I think he has been unfair in not giving me due credit. He may well have adapted cognitive therapy from my early work with REBT. Now his daughter Judith has moved closer to REBT. She follows me by using some forceful vigorous methods. He at first just used cognitive disputing. I think he genuinely believes that he originated cognitive therapy, which is partly true. He may have taken a lot from [my] *Reason and Emotion in Psychotherapy* and my earlier writings. His first paper on cognitive therapy was published in 1963, while *Reason and Emotion in Psychotherapy* and my other books were published before that. So it's too bad. Just like it's too bad other writers made a fortune adapting my writings, without giving me any credit. So I regret that. I'm sorry about it, but I'm not angry and I'm not upset. That happens. People will copy stuff from me (and others) without giving credit, which a forthcoming book edited by Emmett Velten will show in detail. Too bad.

MSB: Unbelievably, you have quite a good attitude about that.

AE: I don't lie awake nights making myself angry!

MSB: Before you broke away from the psychoanalytic establishment you were obviously very frustrated with analysis. Were you frustrated with the inefficiency of it?

AE: That's right. The inefficiency. It was woefully inefficient and sidetracking and I think it very often does much more harm than good, as also do several other therapies.

MSB: What was it like for you when you were still a member of that establishment because that was really the only game in town really at that time and you, a therapist and a psychologist, were there, and you were seeing that the old stuff wasn't working, before you really articulated on the principals of REBT?

AE: I published several papers in the 1940s and 1950s criticizing psychoanalysis for being unscientific. I did my best to make it more scientific, but very few analysts listened to me.

MSB: Was that difficult for you to still be aligned with the analysts and have your innovations falling on deaf ears?

AE: Yes, I felt that they were being ineffectual. I actually wrote a monograph in 1950, when I was still an analyst, showing how to make psychoanalysis scientific. So I disliked what analysts were doing. They were very ineffective and inefficient. But I wasn't upset about it. And then finally in 1953, I stopped calling myself an analyst and called myself a psychotherapist. From 1953 to 1955, I formulated and started REBT.

MSB: Was it a problem for you to leave that establishment? You must have had a lot of relationships there with many colleagues.

AE: It was a problem because a number just accepted my quitting psychoanalysis, but a number were very vituperative and nasty. Don't forget, I was doing analysis but I really wasn't aligned to any group. The American Psychoanalytical Society wouldn't accept psychologists and I was not a member of any other psychoanalytical group. So some analysts hated me and made nasty remarks. But I didn't let that bother me because, again, I don't need other people's approval. I used REBT on myself.

MSB: And again, the secret of being able to do that, which is in a sense what you always come back to, is probably to let other people's negativity roll off you.

AE: Right. And I just concluded that they're different from me and they don't accept me. I wish to hell they would and some of them did, of course. Some of them went along with me, but not very many. Rudolph Dreikurs, the Adlerian, was one of the few outstanding people who saw what I was doing and that it was close to Adlerianism and backed me up. But practically everybody else was against me including Fritz Perls, Carl Rogers, and many other therapists. Too bad! But I thought they were wrong, too. I felt, "I'm more efficient than they are so I'll keep going."

MSB: Now what you are doing is just about as mainstream as it can get to be, I see that there is hardly a gloat there, but you obviously enjoy it.

AE: I like the fact that we're mainstream now, even though cognitive behavior therapy sometimes neglects me and gives credit to Beck and Meichenbaum. But REBT is in the mainstream now. Fine.

MSB: If you had another 45 years to develop this further, where do you think this would go? Is the bulk of the work done?

AE: I think we would continue with research and clinical work, and try to empirically confirm my main theory, which is that absolutistic "musts" and demands largely lead to human disturbance. Beck doesn't accept that, nor does Meichenbaum. So I still think that we had better do some research work to show that when people take their preferences and make them into rigid musts, they upset themselves. Now Stephen Hayes has just come out with a brilliant book, which overlaps with REBT. But he slightly includes the musts in his therapy and doesn't see them as the core philosophies involved in emotional disturbance.

MSB: In fact, there are some people who write about success who will say that in order to be truly successful you have to feel like you *must* be successful.

AE: Right. Some people think that your "musts" help you. I say you could have a very strong preference, but you'd better not have musts or demands. REBT stresses this point while other cognitive behavior therapies still relatively neglect it.

19.

AN EXAMPLE OF WHERE REBT HAS HELPED ME IN MY PERSONAL LIFE

Iused to be quite angry at people who acted stupidly and/or immorally and at "horrible" world conditions. My use of REBT on myself, when I started to apply it to others in January 1955, convinced me that my angry feelings were largely created by my absolutistic demands that people *must* treat me fairly and considerately and were "rotten people" when they didn't. I taught many of my clients unconditional other-acceptance (UOA), to accept the sinner but not the sins, and thereby to refuse to feel angry.

I got a chance to put my unconditional other-acceptance into practice in 1993, when I was celebrating my eightieth birthday. For several years before that, I had been collaborating on a book with a close friend. I gave my collaborator considerable material that I had already gathered for the book, and he promised to complete it in, at most, a year, and by doing so get some credit on his PhD.

However, after three years and still no finished manuscript, the publisher rightly canceled the contract for the book, and it never was published.

Under ordinary conditions, before I began to use REBT on myself, I would have been incensed for several reasons: (1) My collaborator was procrastinating. (2) He was not honest about the work he was doing. (3) He had me write a special letter to his university saying that he was working hard on the book. (4) I had agreed to forgive him $8,000 he owed me when he completed the book; but after the publisher canceled our contract, he stated that I had forgiven the money he owed me just for *starting* to work on the book. So he canceled the debt.

Instead of making myself incensed, I used REBT to make myself feel very displeased with his *behavior* but not angry at *him*. How? By telling myself, "Too bad that he has lied, cheated, and procrastinated, but that rotten *behavior* doesn't make him a *bad person*." I no longer viewed him as a close friend but was not angry at him. I invited him to my eightieth birthday party in 1993 and we talked in a pleasant manner, reminisced about some of our mutual experiences over the years, and semi-humorously mentioned our monetary differences. No, no feelings of anger, rancor, or resentment on my part. By using REBT and its philosophy and practice on myself, I accepted his poor behavior and I rarely think anymore of the highly immoral way he treated me. When he died a couple of years ago, I fondly remembered the many good things we had done together.

20.

COPING WITH MY DIVORCES

My divorces from Karyl and Rhoda and my separation from Janet after living with her for thirty-seven years were not very difficult at first but became more difficult with Rhoda and Janet partly for practical reasons.

With Karyl, at the age of twenty-four, I had nothing to lose—no money, no steady job, and no helping profession to be criticized for not following. Karyl, as I had noted, suggested our marrying when I told her I loved but no longer needed her. She greatly admired that and proposed marriage. As a strong experimentalist who thought marriage might not work out, I agreed to try it and see.

Because I was soon to end my job working for my father's bridge game business, and Karyl had exhausted her WPA Theatre stay and had no acting work, we agreed that our marriage would be entirely secret for a while (till our finances improved). Otherwise, always money oriented, her parents would have exploded. So we secretly went to Hoboken for our first papers on Monday and were about to close the deal on Thursday, when I got a call to come over to Karyl's apartment *immediately.* She had (idiotically!) told her parents we were about to be married. Karyl: "I just can't keep it in!" Whether she could not was debatable; but the fact that "she didn't keep it in" wasn't.

When I got to Karyl's apartment, her parents, despite her father's serious cardiac condition, screamed for an hour. "How could you! You [Karyl] were feebleminded! You obviously can't go ahead with it!"

I saw that there was no use arguing with them. None! So I asked if Karyl and I could go in the other room for a few minutes to talk this over. They knew there was only one possible answer: we would completely agree *not* to go through with this "insanity."

I immediately said to Karyl in the other room, "Too bad you told them. They now won't listen to anything we could say. So I suggest that we tell them we're calling the whole thing off and then go anyway tomorrow to Hoboken and get married. But *this* time, you have to promise to shut your mouth!"

Karyl, stunned, hardly knew what to say. But within five minutes, she agreed that a lesser evil by far was to promise her parents not to marry and then shut up about actually marrying. She learned her lesson from their outburst. She wanted to (peacefully!) marry—and would definitely shut up about doing so.

So we promised Karyl's parents not to marry and went to

Hoboken the next afternoon and (rather somberly and joylessly!) got married. The justice of the peace who married us was quite cheerful, but not us.

You'd really think that would end it. No. When I called to see Karyl that night, she quietly informed me that she *again* had told her parents of the marriage. They had insisted that we immediately *had* to get a divorce. She had agreed to do so, and as a matter of fact (what a fact!) she was leaving her parents' apartment in a couple of hours to (would you believe it?) start living with Ronald Fivis, with whom she had been erratically infatuated for several months!

I wasn't *too* surprised or shocked. By now I didn't trust Karyl at all for *anything* that she might do. I calmly agreed with her that yes, we would immediately go for a divorce and she and I would still be friends. Ronald, I thought, would really suffer from living with a "total screwball" like Karyl. On the contrary, I was now free, thoroughly free!

I meant it. Karyl was "hopelessly screwy" and needed a great deal of professional help, and I was lucky for such a denouement. As for my still being in love with Karyl, I would fix *that*.

I think I did. For the next few months, I befriended Karyl (and Ron), helped them with their (enormous) difficulties, and truly gave up on being madly in love with Karyl. I still loved her for some of her charming (and erratic) qualities, but was mainly happy that I (certainly) didn't need her and could relinquish all responsibilities for taking care of her.

Actually, I didn't quite do that. It's a long story quite fit for my autobiography, but *very* briefly: I remained quite friendly (including sexually friendly) with Karyl; helped her survive

Ronald for several months; gave her supportive rational therapy when Ronald left her a few months later to live with his ex-girlfriend in China; helped her over her depressive breakdown; lived with her (after our annulment) for a year; decided she was too crazy (and sometimes suicidal) for me; helped her get another boyfriend (whom she later married); and was very friendly to her for the rest of her life (until she died at age eighty-three) when I was eighty-eight.

At the time Karyl first told her parents we were about to marry, how did I feel about her dependently doing so? I was surprised that she told them, but I understood her severe dependency and accepted *her* with *it*. I felt no real anger, but rather irritation at her behavior.

How did I feel about the horror of being a son-in-law (without money)? I felt irritated, again, about her parents' disturbances, but not angry at them. The not-so-old codgers were doing what I expected them to do—and would do it forever. Rough! I didn't *want* them as in-laws but was quite prepared for the worst. If anything, their horrified reactions helped to make me more convinced than ever to go ahead and marry Karyl because *we* wanted to do so and to resolve to ignore them as in-laws. Then, when Karyl and I decided to get a quick divorce, I was relieved to rid myself of them forever!

Actually, we didn't get a divorce but an annulment. My lawyer said this would be easier to obtain if we were married for only a short while. So we concocted a story to back up an annulment. I would lie and claim to be a very religious Jew, with whom Karyl promised to have a religious ceremony right after our civil marriage. She practically swore that she would do so—in front of my "deeply religious" mother.

Right after the marriage, she categorically stated to my mother and me that she was an atheist, and certainly would never marry me religiously. I (and my poor old mother) was horrified and couldn't *possibly* give up a Jewish religious ceremony. So Karyl and I *had* to go for an annulment, else I might kill myself.

It was incredible crap! I had been an atheist since I was twelve, and at this time I was more so than ever. But, in November of the year I married Karyl, we got a court date and I almost won an Oscar for telling the judge and the court how deeply I was depressed at the very thought of Karyl not religiously marrying me and how I absolutely must have this horrible marriage annulled on the perfectly legal grounds of Karyl's having married me fraudulently, since her lie substantially forced me into marrying her.

The court was utterly determined to end this case quickly. "Get on with your plaintiff's case fast!" the judge told one lawyer who was asking for his client's annulment because of her refusal to consummate her marriage and was giving too many details. "We haven't got all day!"

My lawyer was less lackadaisical. Within a few minutes, he had me testify to Karyl's perfidy, my mother backed me up, and the annulment was granted. Technically, I had never even been married. And Karyl's parents had never been my in-laws. Good riddance.

As I briefly noted above, I then remained very friendly with Karyl and Ron, especially with Ron, so I could help him live with Karyl till we were officially annulled. She was a tough customer and Ron started to leave her every week but stayed two more months, until he finally escaped to China.

I then experimentally lived with Karyl for a year, knowing that I would leave as soon as she stopped being suicidal. We got along well, had some pretty good sex, and fortunately she was out every night with friends and lovers—most of whom were as disturbed as she and who just weren't my cup of tea.

One notable thing happened when Karyl went to a gynecologist who diagnosed her as being vaginally too tight for intercourse with anyone. He recommended vaginal surgery and put her on dilators for two months. That worked to "loosen her up," and we were going to have "real" intercourse for the first time when she suddenly took a new "handsome" lover and asked my permission to have a date with him one Saturday night.

I was "naturally" jealous. After all, I had waited for two years to take Karyl's technical virginity. Actually, she was probably the most promiscuous virgin in New York! But, on theoretical grounds, I gave her permission to see her new boyfriend that Saturday, because I was busily engaged on my momentous *Case for Sexual Promiscuity* in which I held "free love" was better than "puritanical love," because it gave complete freedom to *any* couple who agreed with each other to have polygamous sex.

Knowing that Karyl, who was finally ready for intercourse, would have it this first time with Kermit, instead of me, I gave her permission to have it. I stayed in our apartment working on my book but actually working on my jealousy till 1:00 AM, when Karyl returned from her date with Kermit. "Yes," she said, "Intercourse was all right. Slightly painful, but all right. No, I didn't have an orgasm."

I was really delighted. With my theory of promiscuity I had made it, by thinking of Karyl's having sex with Kermit, and definitely *not* upsetting myself about it. My "free love" theory could actually work! I was glad for Karyl—and her successful loss of her virginity. And I was enthusiastic for me—who had proved that I could unjealously permit Karyl to freely have me *and* different partners. It worked. Now I *knew* I could have "free love" with women for the rest of my life.

It wasn't that I was "faithful" to Gertrude, Rhoda, Alma, and other women for the rest of my life mainly because I was too busy to take time out for affairs. I allowed my women to have lovers or husbands and I was amazingly unjealous. With Janet, I had my own share of brief affairs—she even *arranged* one of them herself. But I easily accepted her more frequent ones, some of them torrid. I even *liked* the fact that my beloveds were nonmonogamous, like one of my correspondents that I write about in my book, *Sex without Guilt in the Twentieth Century*. He *enjoyed* allowing his partner to have sex-love freedom. So did I.

I have already told about my sad breakup with Gertrude after six years of ideal romantic love. Now to my divorce from Rhoda, with whom I was passionately in love for about a year and lived with another year and a half during which we both had nightly and stupendously frequent orgasms. But I saw innumerable REBT clients during the week, worked on many articles and books (largely on weekends), started my career as a frequent lecturer and workshop presenter, and did various other things. Meanwhile, Rhoda was almost as busy, teaching dance and movement, working at Manhattan State Hospital, studying with Alvin Nikolai and Hanya Holm, and having several special friends, relatives, and lovers. We never quarreled, got along beautifully, and enjoyed our living together arrangement. But I didn't enjoy our Sundays, mainly spent with Rhoda's boring friends. It was a waste of time. Nor did I enjoy all of the modern ballets we attended. I am more enthusiastic about classical ballet.

I might well have continued our "good" marriage but Rhoda fell in love with a male dancer; and she also broke her foot, so that she was able to dance in only a limited manner. She had made her time for socializing—but not I. She decided to end our marriage and we had an amicable divorce. We remained good friends (to this day). I helped her with her next marriage (to Murray Russell, a urologist) and counseled her during her separation from him when he died a few years later. I still am fond of her but was quite intimate with several other women (one of whom, Alma, I lived with for a year) until I met and started living with Janet, when she was twenty-four and I was fifty-one—thirty-seven eventful years—which I have written about elsewhere in this book.

To summarize: I have had two marriages, two living together arrangements (LTAs), many passionate love experiences, and scores of (relatively brief) sexual affairs from my twenty-fourth to my ninetieth year. In a sense, they made me what I am today. I don't strongly regret any of them since I learned much about myself and others (including in-laws!) in the course of them.

I have to watch it, however. Since 1943, I have been a well-known sex, love, and marital relationship counselor voted by members of the American Association of Marital & Family Therapists in the 1980s as the fourth-most-influential writer. Therefore, when therapists and clients briefly hear about my love and marital "record," they sometimes conclude that I have "trouble" relating to women and am not to be trusted to counsel maritally inclined people. "False!" I say on several counts because I have probably helped more relating people than almost any other therapist and writer. But I still have to cope with the evaluations of many people who think otherwise. I try to use their prejudiced conclusions to learn from them and increase my usefulness to single and married people who have problems. But, as usual, I don't take views of my detractors *too* seriously; and I continue on my merry way. So some people don't trust me as a helper in the dating, marrying, and relating field. I am disappointed but I carry on!

21.

AN EXAMPLE WHERE REBT HAS NOT PERSONALLY WORKED FOR ME

Normally, I have fairly high frustration tolerance (HFT), which I have increased over the years by using REBT on myself. This is evidenced by my publishing more than seventy-five books and some eight hundred articles, giving over eighty professional and public workshops a year in New York and throughout the world, regularly supervising ten interns and therapists in REBT, and having sessions every week with about seventy individual and group therapy clients. Pretty good for an old man! In fact, in my eighty-ninth year, I published five new books and more than a dozen articles. So I hardly indulge in my natural low frustration tolerance (LFT) and procrastination, but make strong efforts to override them.

Nonetheless, I still at times suffer from abysmal LFT—and my use of REBT hardly removes it. Take, for example, what happened to me in August 1999. I was scheduled to give workshops from 10:00 AM to 5:00 PM in Colorado Springs. To make sure I arrived in time, I planned on taking a flight on one of the largest airlines from New York directly to Colorado Springs the afternoon before. We were scheduled to leave New York at 5:00 PM, stop over briefly in Dallas, and then arrive at our destination at 9:00 PM. I deliberately took this flight because it was the only one that went, with an interim stop, directly to Colorado Springs. So, presumably, I couldn't miss getting there Thursday night, in good time to be fresh for my workshops on Friday.

No such luck. The airline never told us passengers what happened to our plane, but after a two-hour delay, the airline finally got us on a substitute plane that was to leave LaGuardia Airport at 7:00 PM. Then, during our delay in taking off, a thunderstorm occurred while we were about to leave LaGuardia. All plane traffic was halted, and we finally left New York at 9:00 PM—several hours late.

The pilots did their best, but by the time we arrived in Dallas, it was midnight Dallas time, so the airline quite unethically, I thought, canceled our continuing flight to Colorado Springs. We were stuck for the night in Dallas. I explained to the airline agent that I had to open my workshop in Colorado Springs at 10:00 AM the next morning and therefore had to have an early flight to that city. He lied to me, said there was no early morning flight and that I would have to take an 11:00 AM flight and arrive, at the earliest, at 12:15 PM, long after my workshop was scheduled to begin. Actually, there was a 6:30 AM flight from Dallas to Colorado Springs, but because it was on a rival airline the agent wrongly told me it didn't exist. So he put me up in a flea-bag hotel for the night in Dallas and cooked my goose good! Not only was the hotel third rate, but about a hundred small ants were crawling on the floor of my bathroom. I spent a good deal of the night killing them.

Fortunately, I called the people for whom I was giving the workshops in Colorado Springs; they got on the phone to the airlines, and I was able to get on a plane at 6:30 AM for Denver and then on to Colorado Springs—for an extra $550 (and after about three hours of sleep on Thursday night). I arrived at my conference at 10:30 AM, so I still missed some of my workshop time. But at least I gave most of my presentations.

To make matters still worse, I was supposed to fly on Friday night, after my workshops, back to New York on the same delinquent airline that had unethically given me so much trouble on Thursday. As a result of their poor scheduling, they gave me only forty-five minutes to connect in Denver with my New York leg, and my leg to Denver was a half-hour late. I had to run a fantastic distance at the Denver airport to catch my New York plane. I, and my bedraggled luggage, finally made the New York plane, just as they were closing the doors to take off. I was lucky and the last one to make the plane.

What frustrations on this trip, for which this well-known airline was reprehensibly responsible. Thus: (1) My original plane got unexpectedly lost. (2) We were therefore two hours late in starting. (3) We consequently sat on the field another hour waiting for a thunderstorm to pass. (4) We were three hours late to Dallas. (5) The airline unethically canceled our duly scheduled flight to Colorado Springs—for no good reason that I could see. (6) The agent lied to me about there being no early flight Friday morning to my destination. (7)

The airline put me up for the night in a flea-bag motel, which had hundreds of ants in the bathroom.

Frankly, I was incensed. I obsessively awfulized. I tried to use my best REBT, but it didn't work. I foolishly vowed to never use that infamous airline again. My usual high frustration tolerance failed me and for two days, including my trip back to New York and the following day, I inwardly seethed. As soon as I returned, I wrote the airline a scathing note and demanded monetary remuneration.

Finally, I went over the dismal events of the trip, saw that the airline was wrong and its unethical agent was highly fallible, but that those kinds of mistakes were not *horrible* and sometimes inevitably occurred. I then got back some measure of my higher frustratioin tolerance. I damned the *behavior* of the airline and its agent, but stopped blaming the airline *itself* or the personhood of the agent. At last, my REBT began to work again. I have even traveled on that wrongheaded airline again since that time, with, fortunately, much better results. My ill-fated trip was indeed bad but I could *stand* it, learn from it, and still survive. My frustration tolerance was, for a while, rudely interrupted—but not forever.

22.

MY PHILOSOPHY
OF SEX REVOLUTION

Before I tell how I blended my philosophic outlook with REBT, let me give some relevant details of how I first used philosophy with the revolutionary outlook of sex theory and practice. As I have noted, by the time I got deeply involved with Karyl, when I was twenty-four, I was already withdrawing from the collectivist political activity, helped by Stalin's fanatical despotism. But being, I guess, a real revolutionist at heart, I went directly into sexual revolution more than ever, and quickly became, along with a few people like LeMon Clark, Bertrand Russell, Walter Robie, and A. P. Pillay, a full-force general sex revolutionist. I was a new American editor of the *International Journal of Sexology* and wrote volubly in favor of clitoral orgasm in women, women's sexual rights, free love, and sexual liberation of children, among other topics.

I also founded the Society for the Scientific Study of Sex (SSSS) with Hans Lehfeldt, Hugo Beigel, Robert Sherwin, and other sex liberals. Typically, however, I was *too* liberal for many of my colleagues. Though I was clearly entitled to be the first president of the SSSS, my friend Hans Lehfeldt said I was too "dangerous" for this position, and he almost blocked me from getting it. But I was barely voted in and began to push the SSSS more than ever. It eventually became the outstanding group of its kind and has made sex research quite acceptable. Many of its members still think I am too radical and block my influence (but I don't let them block my views too much). On goes the Sexual Revolution!

23.

SEQUENCE OF THE MAIN EVENTS OF ALBERT ELLIS'S RECENT EXPERIENCES WITH SERIOUS HEALTH AILMENTS

I, Debbie Joffe, have been assisting Albert Ellis and have been in Fellowship training at the Institute, and shall now give my eyewitness account of what happened to Al from late May to August 2003.

Al's schedule for 2003 was very full, including travel plans he had made for his giving workshops and presenting at conferences around the country. In New York he was seeing clients, leading four therapy groups, supervising interns and Fellows at the institute, writing books and articles, and giving his famous Friday night workshop each week.

It was the final week of May 2003. No one anticipated what was to come. . . .

Friday May 30 was another busy Albert Ellis day, seeing clients, meeting with Jigme Norbu (the nephew of the Dalai

Lama) to arrange Al's participation in an event in September with His Holiness the Dalai Lama, and giving a lively Friday night workshop. Though Al had some diarrhea, he didn't suffer from it nor complain about it. The next day Al phoned me, saying his diarrhea was continuing and that he had vomited a few times. When I got to the Institute, I felt alarmed to see how pale and unwell he looked. The only available visiting physician assistant I could find was not able to see Al till the next day because of brutal weather and dangerous travel conditions. I stayed at the Institute through the night to observe Al and to make sure his condition didn't get worse.

The physician assistant arrived mid-afternoon on Sunday. Though Al's blood sugar was high, she initially suggested that he stick to a tea/toast/bananas diet for the diarrhea, and said that things would probably settle. As she was leaving, Al vomited. She said, "All things considered, let's be safe. Get Al to the hospital."

There were two large street parades going on that afternoon, and I could not find any available cabs. Al was looking paler by the minute, so I called for an ambulance. With its siren wailing, it wove through thick traffic and got to one of the leading New York hospitals as quickly as possible. Within twenty minutes of arriving at the emergency room, Al was passing black feces, then blood and fecal matter, and still more blood. This continued uncontrollably for hours.

There appeared to be an insufficient nursing staff that day. Often, staff at the hospital did not respond to Al's calls for help, and they became aggressive with me when I asked for their help for him.

All day on Sunday and Monday Al endured tests, x-rays, CAT

scans, more tests, probes, and needles. The painful exploration procedures seemed endless. His courage was awe inspiring.

By Tuesday June 3 it was determined that Al's colon had to be removed because it was severely infected. If it had burst, and it was treacherously close to doing so, Al would have died.

Post-operation: On Wednesday June 4, Al slept deeply for some hours. He occasionally would wake and give a smile. Little did we know that too much pain-killing medication was entering his body through a drip, and a few hours later he was having severe respiratory problems. He was rushed to intensive care.

Another close call!

Thursday morning Al woke, initially disoriented and agitated. His vital signs were better, though his white-blood-cell count remained exceedingly high. As he regained clarity, he asked me to ask him questions. The interview that resulted was sent to Al's friends, colleagues, and associates. Here it is:

While sitting by Al's bed in the ICU on June 5, 2003, two days after major surgery to remove his colon, the morning after he had been moved to intensive care in a very precarious condition with respiratory difficulty, Al said, "Ask me questions."

DJ: What sort of questions, Al?

AE: Questions people might want to ask me.

DJ: Okay then. What would you say to people who feel afraid about what happened and about your condition?

AE: That it doesn't do them any good to be afraid. Say, "I hope to hell he's well, but if he isn't, he isn't. Fuck it."

DJ: What was your experience like when you were told that you needed to have surgery?

AE: I thought, "Too damned bad—so I'll have it." I felt real concern, because anything could happen and I'd wished the doctors had said no surgery was needed. But they said it was, so I accepted what I couldn't change and thought about things to do now, that is, immediate practical concerns.

DJ: What do you want your friends, colleagues, students, and clients to know about this situation?

AE: Know the truth, and nothing but the truth. I've had serious surgery, but I'll be returning soon to the Institute, to work for another ninety years in all probability!

DJ: What was the predominant emotion that you felt after the operation?

AE: Concern, but not too much. I was thinking, "Back to work." But my concern was that maybe there will be too much work to do right now.

DJ: Did you adopt any humor to help you through this time?

AE: Yes, I thought of a few humorous things, though I can't remember them right now.

(Debbie's note: Soon after Al heard that his colon had to be removed he said, "At least they're not taking my balls!")

DJ: What has been the greatest help to you at this time?

AE: Just to know that people will push their asses, push their asses, to help me and the cause of the Institute. Many people say they'll support us. Let's see if they do. But if they don't, they don't. Too damned bad!

DJ: Describe the cause of the Institute.

AE: That would take too long to answer fully. But briefly, the cause of the Institute is to show people that *they* mainly upset themselves about whatever bad things happen. The bad things that happen don't merely, by themselves, upset people. They control their *attitude* toward these unfortunate events.

DJ: Any final thoughts that you want to share?

AE: I appreciate the support of everyone at the Institute and my friends. If all do their best, I'll get through this, and even they can get through this if they take the REBT approach.

Yet another CAT scan was needed in order to identify the cause of Al's high white-blood-cell count. There continued to be insufficient nursing staff to attend to Al's needs. His blood sugar levels were not being checked often enough, despite my constant requests, urging, and battling with the staff to do so.

On Friday at 3:30 AM we went down to radiology for the CAT scan. Only two staff members were there, and they were attending to another patient. One of them asked me to give Al some barium solution to drink, prior to the procedure. I could not arouse Al to consciousness. He had fallen into a coma. I screamed for a doctor. Within minutes one arrived and a glucose drip was immediately arranged. Al was revived.

Another *very* close call! After this event, we arranged for hired agency nurses to care for Al, to supplement the insufficient hospital care. Unfortunately some of the hired nurses were at times negligent.

Al bravely endured his continuing pain and discomfort, but he lost interest in food. He would force himself to take in some of it, but it at best had no flavor, and at worst was quite "awful."

By about June 19, there was some improvement, and Al was moved to the rehabilitation unit of the hospital to get him out of bed more and to be more active.

On Wednesday June 25, Al returned to the Institute! Two days later he gave a three-hour workshop to doctoral students visiting from Philadelphia. Though weak, Al gave a brilliant presentation and answered questions in a lively way.

Despite Al's struggling to eat and consultations with his doctors and a nutritionist, he continued to get weaker. One of the medications he'd been given to combat itchiness caused Al to feel heavily drowsy. I spoke to a doctor who approved Al's coming off this drug. (Always ask about side effects of medication!) Al's alertness improved after the termination of this medication.

On Friday, July 11, Al gave a two-and-a-half-hour lecture to the Institute's summer Fellows on the evolution of REBT, and that evening he gave a great Friday night workshop, despite his feeling weak. His blood sugar levels were extremely erratic, and I observed that his low energy and weakness was increasing alarmingly.

Because two of the agency nurses, who attended to him around the clock, were, in my view, not not too careful, Al was not getting sufficient hydration and nutrition, however one did agree that we'd better get him to his main doctor quickly.

We took a cab there. Al's white-blood-cell count was extremely high again. Off to the hospital's emergency room we went—immediately.

Al was severely dehydrated. No source of infection was found. It was hypothesized that perhaps blood was oozing from the surgical site (internally), and Al's body mistook that as being intrusive foreign organisms to fight. Hence the elevated white-blood-cell count.

A new caring team of nurses was found for Al. On Wednesday July 23, Al returned home. He began eating and drinking more. His energy levels increased gradually. On Friday, July 25,

Al gave a workshop on anxiety to the summer Fellows—in his bedroom!

Over the weekend, his alertness increased, he read more and wrote more. The following week he did the Friday night workshop, and he has resumed doing it each week since.

Al's surgeon felt that it would not be advisable for him to travel to the August American Psychological Association's meeting in Toronto, where he was scheduled for six presentations. In any case, most were canceled because of the SARS dangers that kept people away. Al did however participate in two of his scheduled sessions by phone.

At the time of my writing this, Al continues to improve in terms of his strength and energy. I am incredibly fortunate to observe his remarkable qualities throughout this challenging time in his life, and the way he stubbornly pushes to get better in order to continue his REBT Institute causes. Nothing seems to stop him—not even his fragile health.

24.

THE CARE YOU EXPECT
AND THE CARE YOU GET
WHEN YOU ARE REALLY AILING

W hat kind of care should you preferably get and what kind are you likely to receive when you are really ill or disabled? I frankly don't remember much of what happened when I spent ten months in the Presbyterian Hospital when I had nephritis from five to nine years of age, but I thought I was treated well. People were kind and considerate, including the nurses, and I suffered only a bit of neglect from my parents. I was often lonely but hardly abused.

Later I had some brief hospitalizations for a major prostectomy (when I was sixty-six) and again for a broken collarbone. Still later, I had a major operation for a twisted stomach (when I was seventy-five). As far as I can remember, people were kind and caring, and my medical and nursing care was excellent at these times.

I was little prepared therefore for my colonectomy, which took place in June 2003 when I was approaching ninety. I had severe diarrhea—and very bad itching for several months before that—and high-blood-sugar counts, but no one seemed to suspect that a colonectomy was needed.

Debbie gave me the bad news that whether I liked it or not I would be under twenty-four-hour-a-day nursing for at least a while after the operation. My work was cut almost to zero for a while, and who knew how much of it I would soon be able to do again.

Not working was seemingly a disaster. I went from almost full functioning to near zero and for an indefinite period of time.

I didn't mind the iliostomy which followed the colonectomy because it was done when I was in intensive care and heavily sedated. Since I had a catheter in me I didn't need to get out of bed to urinate; and with the iliostomy I didn't have to defecate, and this had its advantages. I did mind the constant nursing, some of which was cruel and careless. It also led to mistakes in medication—such as giving me too much insulin, which was very dangerous. But little could be slowly done to change things, so I just suffered pain and steady itching—which was often worse than the pain.

Eventually, I got a team of Irish nurses, who were much more competent than the American team, so I survived that. I especially disliked the stupidity, cruelty, and apathy of my first nursing team but had to endlessly put up and shut up about it. Debbie was driven frantic trying to improve things and because of her unusual love for me, and immense caring, she suffered far more than I did. Her tears were often falling. I never thought that I would find a more loving and sweeter person. Without her, I probably would have died. Philip Miller, Emmett Velten, Michael Broder, Kristene Doyle, and others helped considerably, but some Institute people didn't and sometimes blocked Debbie's incredible caring and kindness.

Debbie, I, and others pushed for good results and they got decidedly better. Following my good and bad experiences, I formulated some ideas and procedures that may be useful for other people seriously disabled by accidents, illnesses, or other handicaps. Many or most of these ailing people may be considerably helped if they take the following attitudes and actions. (I'm sure I shall later think of even more they can adopt.)

1. Be ready for anything, yes anything, that may or may not happen. In July 1999 I was already beset with serious diarrhea and itching of unknown origin and I walked with a cane, I had arthritis of my right knee and I had trembly legs and could walk only limited distances. But I never expected that I would mainly be resting in bed all day and be helped by two full-time nurses for twenty-four hours each day. What miserable luck!

2. Be prepared for unusual expenses. Nursing may be very expensive but so too may be physicians, medications, surgery, etc. Your usual income from the work you do could be cut down considerably. Try to be well insured for expenses and for loss of income. Now that you are not yet afflicted, look at your insurance coverage in case you are afflicted.

3. Have you a good support group? Relatives, friends, colleagues, and others? Perhaps you should think about this before you are afflicted.

4. Follow physicians' and nurses' rules even when they seem very strict. They are probably for your good.

5. Different physicians and the rules they set may clash with each other. Some in particular may be harmful to you. Check them!

6. Get as much exercise as you can—especially if you are bedridden.

7. Get physical rehabilitation if it is available.

8. Naturally, I recommend using the main principles and practices of REBT. First, practice unconditional self-acceptance (USA) even if you foolishly brought on some of your ailments—as I probably did by taking on too much to do when I was already in physical trouble. With USA, I blamed my behavior but not myself. Self-damnation wouldn't make things better!

9. Even when other people are responsible for some of your troubles, denigrating them would hardly help them change. So blame their *sins* but not their *selves*. Give them unconditional other-acceptance (UOA).

10. Maybe some *aspects* of your world are truly bad but not your world as a *whole*. Keep that in mind!

11. What are you going to learn from your past, present, and potential future? That is what may really help you and others.

12. What can you do to help yourself and others as a result of your experiences? You won't save the world but may do some considerable good if you forgive and forget.

13. Do any *general* rules of good health follow from your and other people's views and actions about what you prefer-ably should do about your afflictions? Look for them!

Now that I think of it, what were some of the things I did and to which I reacted badly during my affliction? How could I learn from them to help others and myself in the present and future?

1. I was often too impatient and tried to cut corners quickly, which didn't help much. Thus, I forced down less of the rotten but nutritious food that might have helped me had I been more patient and worked on my LFT about it.

2. I was sometimes cross with my nurses and friends when they tried to help me do the "right" things.

3. I did some whining and screaming about the bad things that hindered me from focusing on or trying to improve them. For example, I failed to use some of the distraction and rehabilitation techniques I invented. At least these would have eased my pains. I could have spent more time inventing and using other palliative methods.

4. I didn't usually indulge in debilitating self-pity but still engaged in it sometimes.

5. I was sometimes too pessimistic rather than truly *realistic* about my future. At the same time, I was rarely unrealistically optimistic.

6. I was sometimes too critical of my helpers' "stupidity" and "foolishness" but at least usually kept my impatience and nastiness to myself.

7. I hated much of the "idiocy" of various "helpers" and officials but had the good sense to keep silent about this.

8. When I felt cross with Debbie—which was rare—I usually went out of my way to be silent or say something

nice to her. On the whole I kept reminding myself about how incredibly good, caring, and helpful she was. No nonsense!

9. Even when encountering very unhelpful and unkind actions from a few people, I practically never hated them, only what they did.

10. Although nurses kept screwing up and feeding me terrible food, I didn't put them down for this and rarely refused the food.

11. I was mostly exceptionally patient with my blood tests and other painful tests. And even when they were done quite badly by the nurses, I practically never damned them for their incompetence.

On the whole, my track record in dealing with my physical afflictions wasn't too bad. I still suffer from several of them now that I am partially recovered. I still walk with a cane; and my hearing, though improved with hearing aids, will never be the same as it once was.

All this is very frustrating and at times quite handicapping. But it only partly stops me from doing therapy, writing articles and books, lecturing and teaching, enjoying relationships, reading, listening to music, writing songs, and doing other enjoyable pursuits that are and have been my practice for years and years. Thanks to my often using rational emotive behavior therapy on myself, my handicaps (the "hole" in my doughnut) are still there, but my pleasures and creative activities (the enjoyable doughnut itself) are still very much alive. With the help of REBT philosophy and practice, I shall keep working to keep it that way!

APPENDIX

(For readers of this book who would like to use some important aspects to cope with their physical and emotional problems, consult several of the books and articles listed in the Selected References section. The following information, reprinted from an REBT pamphlet, may also be helpful.)

HOW TO MAINTAIN AND ENHANCE YOUR RATIONAL EMOTIVE BEHAVIOR THERAPY GAINS

If you work at using the principles and practices of rational emotive behavior therapy (REBT), you will be able to change your self-defeating thoughts, feelings, and behaviors and feel much better than when you started therapy. Good! But you will also, at times, fall back—and sometimes far back. No one is perfect and practically all people take one step backward to every two or three steps forward. Why? Because that is the nature of humans: to improve, to stop improving at times, and sometimes to backslide.

How can you (imperfectly!) slow down your tendency to fall back? How can you maintain and enhance your therapy goals? Here are some methods that we have tested at the Albert Ellis Institute's clinic in New York and that many of our clients have found effective.

How To Maintain Your Improvement

1. When you improve and then fall back to old feelings of anxiety, depression, or self-downing, try to remind yourself and pinpoint exactly what thoughts, feelings, and behavior you once changed to bring about your improvement. If you again feel depressed, think back to how you previously used REBT to make yourself undepressed. For example, you may remember that:
   a. You stopped telling yourself that you were worthless and that you couldn't ever succeed at getting what you wanted.
   b. You did well in a job or a love affair and proved to yourself that you did have some ability and that you were lovable.
   c. You forced yourself to go on interviews instead of avoiding them and thereby helped yourself overcome your anxiety about them.
   Remind yourself of past thoughts, feelings, and behaviors that you have helped yourself by changing.

2. Keep thinking, thinking, and thinking Rational Beliefs (RBs) or coping statements, such as: "It's great to succeed, but I can fully accept myself as a person and have enjoyable experiences even when I fail!" Don't merely parrot these statements but go over them carefully many times and think them through until you really begin to believe and feel that they are correct.

3. Keep seeking for, discovering, and disputing and challenging your Irrational Beliefs (IBs) with which you are once again upsetting yourself. Take each important Irrational Belief—such as, "I have to succeed in order to be a worthwhile person!"—and keep asking yourself: "Why is this belief true?" "Where is the evidence that my worth to myself, and my enjoyment of living, utterly depends on my succeeding at something?" "How does failing at an important task make me totally unacceptable as a human?"

   Keep forcefully and persistently disputing your Irrational Beliefs whenever you see that you are letting them creep back again. Even when you don't actively hold them, realize that they may arise once more, bring them to your consciousness, and preventively—and vigorously!—dispute them!

4. Keep risking and doing things that you irrationally fear—such as riding in elevators, socializing, job hunting, or creative writing. Once you have partially overcome one of your irrational fears, keep acting against it on a regular basis. If you feel uncomfortable in forcing yourself to do things that you are unrealistically afraid of doing, don't allow yourself to avoid

doing them—or else you'll preserve your discomfort forever! Practice making yourself as uncomfortable as you can be, in order to eradicate your irrational fears and become unanxious and comfortable later.

5. Try to clearly see the real difference between *healthy* negative emotions—such as those of sorrow, regret, and frustration—and *unhealthy* negative feelings, such as depression, anxiety, self-hatred, and self-pity.

Whenever you feel overconcerned (panicked) or unduly miserable (depressed), acknowledge that you are having a statistically normal but a psychologically unhealthy feeling and that you are mainly bringing it on yourself with some dogmatic should, ought, or must.

Realize that you are capable of changing your unhealthy (or *mustur*batory) feelings back into healthy (or preferential) ones. Take your depressed feelings and work on them until you feel only concerned and vigilant. Use rational emotive imagery to vividly imagine unpleasant Activating Events, even before they happen: let yourself feel unhealthily upset (anxious, depressed, enraged, or self-downing) as you imagine them; then work on your feelings to change them to healthy negative emotions (concern, sorrow, annoyance, or regret) as you keep imagining some of the worst things happening. Don't give up until you actually change your feelings.

6. Avoid self-defeating procrastination. Do unpleasant tasks fast—today! If you still procrastinate, reward yourself with certain things that you enjoy—for example, eating, vacationing, reading, and social-

izing—only after you have performed the tasks you easily avoid. If this won't work, give yourself a severe penalty—such as talking to a boring person for two hours or burning a hundred dollar bill—every time you procrastinate.

7. Show yourself that it is an absorbing challenge and something of an adventure to maintain your emotional health and to keep yourself reasonably happy no matter what kinds of misfortunes assail you. Make the uprooting of your misery one of the most important things in your life—something you are utterly determined to steadily work at achieving. Fully acknowledge that you almost always have some choice about how to think, feel, and behave: then throw yourself actively into making that choice for yourself.

8. Remember—and use—the three main insights of REBT that were first outlined in *Reason and Emotion in Psychotherapy* in 1962:

Insight No. 1: You largely choose to disturb yourself about the unpleasant events of your life, although you may be encouraged to do so by external happenings and by social learning. You may feel the way you think. When obnoxious and frustrating things happen to you at Point A (Activating Events or Adversities), you consciously or unconsciously select Rational Beliefs (RBs) that lead you to feel sad and regretful, and you also select Irrational Beliefs (IBs) that lead you to feel anxious, depressed, and self-hating.

Insight No. 2: No matter how or when you acquired your Irrational Beliefs and your self-sabotaging habits, you now, in the present, choose to maintain them—and that is why you are now disturbed. Your past history and your present life conditions importantly affect you; but they don't disturb you. Your present philosophy is the main contributor to your current disturbance.

Insight No. 3: There is no magical way for you to change your personality and your strong tendencies to needlessly upset yourself. Basic personality change requires persistent work and practice—yes, work and practice—to enable you to alter your Irrational Beliefs, your unhealthy feelings, and your self-destructive behaviors.

9. Steadily and unfrantically look for personal pleasures and enjoyments—such as reading, entertainment, sports, hobbies, art, science, and other vital, absorbing interests. Make your major life goal not only the achievement of emotional health but also that of real enjoyment. Try to become involved in a long-term purpose, goal, or interest in which you can remain truly absorbed. A good, happy life will give you something to live for; will distract you from many serious woes; and will encourage you to preserve and improve your mental health.

10. Try to keep in touch with several other people who know something about REBT and who can help you review some of its aspects. Tell them about problems that you have difficulty coping with and let them know how you are using REBT to overcome these problems. See if they agree with your solutions and can suggest

additional and better kinds of disputing that you can use to work against your Irrational Beliefs.

11. Practice using REBT with some of your friends, relatives, and associates who are willing to let you try to help them with it. The more often you use it with others, and are able to see what their IBs are and to try to talk them out of these self-defeating ideas, the more you will be able to understand the main principles of REBT and to use them with yourself. When you see other people act irrationally and in a disturbed manner, try to figure out—with or without talking to them about it—what their main Irrational Beliefs probably are and how these could be actively and vigorously disputed.

12. When you are in REBT individual or group therapy, try to record many of your sessions and listen to these carefully between sessions, so that some of the ideas that you learned in therapy sink in. After therapy sessions, play these recordings back to yourself from time to time to remind you how to deal with some of your old problems or new ones that may arise.

13. Keep reading rational writings and listening to REBT audio- and videocassettes.

How to Deal with Backsliding

1. Accept your backsliding as normal—as something that happens to almost all people who at first improve emotionally. See it as part of your human fallibility. Don't

make yourself feel ashamed when some of your old symptoms return; and don't think that you have to handle them entirely by yourself and that it is wrong or weak for you to seek some additional sessions of therapy and to talk to your friends about your renewed problems.

2. When you backslide, look at your self-defeating behavior as bad and unfortunate; but refuse to put yourself down for engaging in this behavior. Use the highly important REBT principle of refraining from rating you, yourself, or your being but of measuring only your acts, deeds, and traits. You are always a person who acts well or badly—and never a good person nor a bad person. No matter how badly you fall back and bring on your old disturbances again, work at fully accepting yourself with this unfortunate or weak behavior—and then try, and keep trying, to change your behavior.

3. Go back to the ABCs of REBT and clearly see what you did to fall back to your old symptoms. At A (Activating Event or Adversity), you usually experienced some failure or rejection. At Rational Belief (RB) you probably told yourself that you didn't like failing and didn't want to be rejected. If you stayed with these Rational Beliefs, you would merely feel sorry, regretful, disappointed, or frustrated. But if you felt disturbed, you probably then went on to some Irrational Beliefs (IBs), such as: "I must not fail! It's horrible when I do!" "I have to be accepted, because if I'm not that makes me an unlovable, worthless person!" If you reverted to these IBs, you probably felt, at C (Emotional Consequence) once again depressed and self-downing.

4. When you find your Irrational Beliefs by which you are once again disturbing yourself, just as you originally used Disputing (D) to challenge and surrender them, do so again—immediately and persistently. Thus, you can ask yourself: "Why must I not fail? Is it really horrible if I do?" And you can answer: "There is no reason why I must not fail, though I can think of several reasons why it would be highly undesirable. It's not horrible if I do fail—only distinctly inconvenient."

   You can also Dispute your other Irrational Beliefs by asking yourself, "Where is it written that I have to be accepted? How do I become an unlovable, worthless person if I am rejected?" And you can answer: "I never have to be accepted, though I would very much prefer to be. If I am rejected, that makes me, alas, a person who is rejected this time by this individual under these conditions, but it hardly makes me an unlovable, worthless person who will always be rejected by anyone for whom I really care."

5. Keep looking for, finding, and actively and vigorously Disputing your Irrational Beliefs to which you have once again relapsed and which are now making you feel anxious or depressed. Keep doing this, over and over, until you build intellectual and emotional muscle (just as you would build physical muscle by learning how to exercise and then by continuing to exercise).

6. Don't fool yourself into believing that if you merely change your language you will always change your thinking. If you neurotically tell yourself, "I *must* suc-

ceed and be approved," and you change this self-statement to "I *prefer* to succeed and be approved," you may still really be convinced, "But I really *have to* do well and be loved." Before you stop your Disputing and before you are satisfied with your answers to it, keep on doing it until you are really convinced of your rational answers and until your feelings of disturbance truly disappear. Then do the same thing, many, many times—until your new E (Effective Philosophy) becomes hardened and habitual—which it almost always will if you keep working at it and thinking it through.

7. Convincing yourself lightly or "intellectually" of your new Effective Philosophy or Rational Beliefs often won't help very much or persist very long. Do so very strongly and vigorously, and do so many times. Thus, you can powerfully convince yourself, until you really feel it: "I do not *need* what I *want*! I never *have to* succeed, no matter how much I *wish* to do so!" "I *can* stand being rejected by someone I care for. It won't *kill* me—and I *still* can lead a happy life!" "No human is damnable and worthless—including me!"

HOW TO GENERALIZE FROM WORKING ON ONE EMOTIONAL PROBLEM TO WORKING ON OTHER PROBLEMS

1. Show yourself that your present emotional problem and the ways in which you bring it on are not unique and that most emotional and behavioral difficulties

are largely created by Irrational Beliefs (IBs). Whatever your IBs are, you can overcome them by strongly and persistently disputing and acting against them.

2. Recognize that you tend to have three major kinds of Irrational Beliefs that lead you to disturb yourself and that the emotional and behavioral problems that you want to relieve fall into one, two, or all three of these categories:

   a. "I *must* do well and *have to* be approved by people whom I find important." This IB leads you to feel anxious, depressed, and self-hating; and will encourage you to avoid doing things at which you may fail or avoiding relationships that may not turn out well.

   b. "Other people *must* treat me fairly and nicely." This IB contributes to your feeling angry, furious, violent, and over-rebellious.

   c. "The conditions under which I live *must* be comfortable and free from major hassles!" This IB tends to bring about feelings of low frustration tolerance and self-pity; and sometimes those of anger and depression.

3. Recognize that when you employ one of these three absolutistic *musts*—or any of the innumerable variations on it—you naturally and commonly derive from them other irrational conclusions, such as:

   a. "Because I am not doing as well I as *must*, I am an incompetent, worthless individual!" (Self-downing)

   b. "Since I am not being approved by people whom I find important, as I *have to* be, it's awful and terrible!" (Awfulizing)

c. "Because others are not treating me as fairly and as nicely as they absolutely *must* treat me, they are utterly rotten people and deserved to be damned!" (Damnation)

d. "Since the conditions under which I live are not that comfortable and since my life has several major hassles, as it *must* not have, *I can't stand it!* My existence is a horror!"(Can't-stand-it-itis)

e. "Because I have failed and gotten rejected as I absolutely *ought not* have done, I'll *always* fail and *never* get accepted as I *must* be! My life will be hopeless and joyless forever!" (Overgeneralizing)

4. Work at seeing that these Irrational Beliefs are part of your general repertoire of thoughts and feelings and that you bring them to many different kinds of situations. Realize that in most cases where you feel seriously upset and act in a self-defeating manner, you are consciously or unconsciously sneaking in one or more of these IBs. Consequently, if you reduce them in one area and are still emotionally disturbed about something else, you can use the same REBT principles to discover your IBs in the new area and to minimize them there.

5. Repeatedly show yourself that you normally won't disturb yourself and remain disturbed if you abandon your absolutistic *shoulds, oughts,* and *musts* and consistently replace them with flexible and unrigid (though still strong) *desires* and *preferences.*

6. Continue to acknowledge that you can change your Irrational Beliefs (IBs) by rigorously (not rigidly!) using realistic and healthy thinking. You can show

yourself that your Irrational Beliefs are only assumption or hypothesis—not facts. You can logically, realistically, and pragmatically Dispute them in many ways such as these:

a. You can show yourself that your IBs are self-defeating—that they interfere with your goals and your happiness. For if you firmly convince yourself, "I *must* succeed at important tasks and *have to* be approved by all the significant people in my life," you will of course at times fail and be disapproved—and thereby inevitably make yourself anxious and depressed instead of sorry and frustrated.

b. Your Irrational Beliefs do not conform to reality—and especially do not conform to the facts of human fallibility. If you always *had to* succeed, if the universe commanded that you *must* do so, you obviously *would* always succeed. But of course you often don't! If you invariably *had to* be approved by others, you could never be disapproved. But obviously frequently you are! The universe is clearly not arranged so that you will always get what you demand. So although your desires are often realistic, your godlike commands definitely are not.

c. Your Irrational Beliefs are illogical, inconsistent, or contradictory. No matter how much you *want* to succeed and to be approved, it never follows that therefore you *must* do well in these (or any other) respects. No matter how desirable justice or politeness is, it never has to exist.

Although REBT disputing is not infallible or sacred, it efficiently helps you to discover which of your beliefs are irrational and self-defeating and how to use realistic, pragmatic, and logical thinking to minimize them. If you keep using flexible thinking, you will avoid dogma and construct your assumptions about you, other people, and world conditions so that you always keep them open to change.

7. Try to set up some main goals and purposes in life—goals that you would like very much to reach but that you never tell yourself that you absolutely *must* attain. Keep checking to see how you are coming along with these goals, and at times revise them. Keep yourself oriented toward the goals that you select and that are not harmful to you or to others. Instead of making yourself extremely self-interested or socially interested, a balanced absorption in both these kinds of goals will often work out best for you and the community in which you choose to live.

8. If you get bogged down and begin to lead a life that seems too miserable or dull, review the points made in this pamphlet and work at using them. If you fall back or fail to go forward at the pace you prefer, don't hesitate to return to therapy for some booster sessions or join one of the Albert Ellis Institute's regular therapy groups.

SELECTED REFERENCES

This is not an academic or professional book, so I shall not give full references to the many articles and books that I have used for many years to think about and to write from. Most of these that I mention in the text are easily available and may be found in bookstores and libraries.

I shall list below only some selected references that you can use if you want to know more about rational emotive behavioral therapy (REBT) and use it in regard to your own handicaps and disabilities or with any of your other problems. Considerable other materials on REBT, as well as workshops and lectures for the public and the profession, are included in our free catalog, which we keep updating every six months.

To get a copy, send your mailing address to or phone the Albert Ellis Institute, 45 East 65th Street, New York, NY 10021. Phone: (212) 535-0822. E-mail: info@rebt.org.

SELECTED REFERENCES

Alberti, R., and R. Emmons. *Your Perfect Right*, 8th ed. Atascadero, CA: Impact, 2001.

Beck, A. T. *Love Is Not Enough*. New York: Harper & Row, 1988.

Bernard, M. E. and J. L. Wolfe, eds. *The REBT Resource Book for Practitioners*. New York: Albert Ellis Institute, 2000.

DiGiuseppe, R. "The Top 10 Reasons to Give Up Your Disturbed Anger." In M. E. Bernard and J. L. Wolfe, eds., *REBT Source Book for Professionals*. New York: Albert Ellis Institute, 2000, pp. iii, 62.

Dryden, W. *Dealing with Anger Problems: Rational-Emotive Therapeutic Interventions*. Sarasota, FL: Professional Resource Exchange, 1990.

———. *Reason to Change: A Rational Emotive Behavior Therapy (REBT) Workbook*. Hove, England: Brunner-Routledge, 2001.

Ellis, A. *How to Live with a "Neurotic": At Home and at Work*. Hollywood, CA: Wilshire Books, 1957 and 1975.

———. "Fun as Psychotherapy." *Rational Living* 12, no. 1 (1977): 2–6. (Also; cassette recording). New York: Albert Ellis Institute, 1977.

———. *A Garland of Rational Humorous Songs*. (Cassette recording and songbook). New York: Albert Ellis Institute, 1977.

———. "Fanaticism That May Lead to Nuclear Holocaust." *Journal of Counseling and Development* 65 (1986): 146–51.

———. *How to Stubbornly Refuse to Make Yourself Miserable About Anything—Yes, Anything!* New York: Kensington Publishers, 1988.

———. *How to Maintain and Enhance Your Rational Emotive Behavior Therapy Gains*. New York: Albert Ellis Institute, 2000.

———. "Spiritual Goals and Spirited Values in Psychotherapy." *Journal of Individual Psychology* 36 (2000): 279–84.

———. *Feeling Better, Getting Better, Staying Better*. Atascadero, CA: Impact, 2001.

———. *Overcoming Destructive Beliefs, Feelings, and Behaviors*. Amherst, NY: Prometheus Books, 2001.

———. *Overcoming Resistance: A Rational Emotive Behavior Therapy Integrated Approach*. New York: Springer, 2002.

————. *Anger—How to Live with and without It.* New York: Citadel Press, 2003.

————. *Ask Albert Ellis.* Atascadero, CA: Impact, 2003.

————. *Sex without Guilt in the Twenty-first Century.* Fort Lee, NJ: Barricade, 2003.

Ellis, A., and T. Crawford. *Making Intimate Connections.* Atascadero, CA: Impact, 2000.

Ellis, A., and J. Gullo. *Murder and Assassination.* New York: Lyle Stuart, 1972.

Ellis, A., and R. A. Harper. *A Guide to Rational Living.* North Hollywood, CA: Melvin Powers, 1997.

————. *How to Stop Destroying Your Relationships.* New York: Citadel, 2001.

Ellis, A., and R. C. Tafrate. *How to Control Your Anger Before It Controls You.* New York: Citadel, 1997.

Hauck, P. A. *Overcoming Frustration and Anger.* Philadelphia: Westminster, 1974.

————. *Overcoming the Rating Game: Beyond Self-Love, Beyond Self-Esteem.* Philadelphia: Westminister, 1992.

His Holiness the Dalai Lama and H. C. Cutler. *The Art of Happiness.* New York: Riverhead, 1998.

Kassinove, H., and R. C. Tafrate. *Anger Management.* Atascadero, CA: Impact, 2002.

Korzybski, A. *Science and Sanity.* Corcord, CA: International Society of General Semantics, 1933 and 1990.

Lange, A., and P. Jakubowski. *Responsible Assertive Behavior.* Champaign, IL: Research Press, 1976.

Novaco, R. *A Treatment Program for the Management of Anger Through Cognitive and Relaxation Controls.* PhD thesis, 1974, Indiana University. Also published as *Anger Control.* Lexington, MA: Lexington Books, 1975.

Phadke, K. M. "Some Innovations in RET Theory and Practice." *Rational Living* 17, no. 2 (1982): 25–30.

SELECTED REFERENCES

Walen, S., R. DiGiuseppe, and W. Dryden. *A Practitioner's Guide to Rational-Emotive Therapy.* New York: Oxford University Press, 1992.

Wolfe, J. L. *What to Do When He Has a Headache.* New York: Hyperion, 1992.

ABOUT THE AUTHOR

Albert Ellis was born in Pittsburgh and raised in New York City. He holds MA and PhD degrees in clinical psychology from Columbia University. He has held many important psychological positions, including Chief Psychologist of the state of New Jersey and adjunct professorships at Rutgers and other universities. He is currently president of the Albert Ellis Institute in New York City; has practiced psychotherapy, marriage and family counseling, and sex therapy for sixty years; and continues this practice at the Psychological Center of the Institute in New York. He is the founder of Rational Emotive Behavior Therapy (REBT), the first of the now popular Cognitive Behavior Therapies (CBT).

Dr. Ellis has served as president of the Division of Consulting Psychology of the American Psychological Association and of the Society for the Scientific Study of Sexuality, and he has also served as officer of several professional societies, including the American Association of Marital and Family Therapy, the American Academy of Psychotherapists, and the American Academy of Sex Educators, Counselors, and Therapists. He is a diplomat in clinical psychology of the American Board of Professional Psychology and of several other professional organizations.

Professional societies that have given Dr. Ellis their highest professional and clinical awards include the American Psychological Association, the Association for the Advancement of Behavior Therapy, the American Counseling Association, and the American Psychopathological Association. He was ranked as one of the "most influential psychologists" by both the American and Canadian psychologists and counselors. He has served as consulting or associate editor of many scientific journals and has published more than eight hundred scientific papers and more than two hundred audio and videocassettes. He has authored or edited more than seventy-five books and monographs, including a number of best-selling popular and professional volumes. Some of his best-known books include *How to Live with a "Neurotic"*; *The Art and Science of Love*; *A Guide to Rational Living*; *Reason and Emotion in Psychotherapy*; *How to Stubbornly Refuse to Make Yourself Miserable about Anything—Yes, Anything*; *Overcoming Procrastination*; *Overcoming Resistance*; *The Practice of Rational Emotive Behavior Therapy*; *How to Make Yourself Happy and Remarkably Less Disturbable*; *Feeling Better, Getting Better, and Staying Better*; *Overcoming Destructive Beliefs, Feelings, and Behaviors*; *Anger: How to Live with It and without It*; and *Sex without Guilt in the Twenty-first Century*.

INDEX